Janet Baker

Alan Blyth

Drake Publishers Inc

NEW YORK

ISBN 0–87749–528–9

Library of Congress Catalog Card No. 73–4709

Published in 1973 by Drake Publishers Inc
381 Park Avenue South, New York, N.Y. 10016

✻ Contents ✻

❧ Introduction ❧

Wherever Janet Baker goes she makes friends. She has that precious boon not granted to or acquired by every artist—the ability instantly to communicate with her audiences. She is herself very well aware of the importance of this gift and emphasises that everything that a singer attempts must have meaning both for the artist and for her audience. "Whatever I'm interpreting —whether it is opera, Lieder, or the *Matthew Passion*—must for that moment be reality, and if you can achieve that, other things will come naturally." She also considers it essential for a fully rounded career to be successful in every field, and to avoid the compartmentalisation that is apt to hamper the careers of British singers. Perhaps she has done more than any other to break down the barriers between the various sectors of musical life: she is now established as not only one of Britain's leading Lieder and oratorio singers, but also one of our finest opera artists.

Janet has achieved her pre-eminence through the conviction and integrity of her career. There has been no sudden flight to the top, no trick or public relations boost through which she has reached her present position. All has been accomplished by hard work and by dedication to her art. Of course, the right engagement at the right time and a record contract have helped, but an artist must have the determination and talent to take those chances, and that she has: also that indefinable quality of presence and dignity without which no amount of talent will carry a singer to the head of her profession. Whether Janet had that quality from the beginning or whether she assumed the mantle on the way up is a matter of conjecture. That she has it now is beyond doubt.

The beginnings were small. So was Janet when she used to sing about the house—in tune, as her mother remembers. Janet's parents were not particularly musical, though her father did sing in church and police choirs near their home at York, and her mother had quite a good voice, but they never commented on Janet's singing at home. When her brother joined the church choir, Janet wanted to join it too. "I remember sitting watching the choir boys and wishing that I could sing with them; eventually the vicar started a ladies' section so when I was about ten I was able to join it. At this age, too, I used to go with my father to the local D'Oyly Carte productions. I recall that I

was very snobbish about that kind of music and the old part-songs the Police Choir used to sing. I thought it was all very well but it wasn't really music. To listen to a Prom on the wireless, well, that was something very different and special. Much of the music I heard—I cannot remember what in particular—moved me very deeply. I felt that this was the real thing."

Janet's father was an engineer. As he was in a reserved occupation in the war, he joined the Special Constabulary and this was how he came to sing in the Police Choir; Janet followed him around with great enthusiasm on a bicycle. She used also to attend the annual choir festivals in York Minster under Edward Bairstow, then the organist. "The sound of all those voices in that setting was unbelievable. But it used to irritate me when people did things badly. When I began to sing in these choirs—I was a high soprano at the time—it annoyed me if somebody next to me did not seem to know what to do with a musical phrase. I was probably a very nasty and arrogant little girl, but the thing was inborn: until then I had no musical training."

❧ Life and Career ❧

When she was thirteen or fourteen, she was given her first piano. "I was dying to have this piano. All my friends could play *Teddy Bears' Picnic* and that used to irritate me, because I thought that that was not what the piano was for. I still feel that many children are put off the piano by being given these awful pieces to learn; they should be able to play good music from the start. Before I got the piano I used to 'play' the sideboard. We had a huge Victorian one that was like an organ so that if there was any music on the radio, I was able to imitate it on the sideboard. I learned the piano until I had to start exams at school, when I dropped it for a couple of years. I took it up again when I was eighteen or so, but I injured my hand when I fell down in a tube train which put an end to my piano playing."

Janet went to a good elementary school. When she was seven or eight, one of her teachers felt that she had some musical talent. "She used to say to me that I was going to be either a singer or a writer. She was quite right. These are the two things that I felt I wanted to do. When she was teaching the class a song, she knew that I would learn it in about two minutes flat, so then she made me sing it to the rest of the class. I remember that that lady had great faith in me from a very early age."

Janet won a scholarship, through her aptitude for English, to York College School, a church establishment attached to the Minster, and next door to the boys' choir school. If her father had not changed his job after the war for one in Grimsby, her course might have been very different; Janet was very unhappy at her new school and almost immediately wanted to move. "I took my exams and then decided I wanted to leave, much against my father's wishes, to study music. Had I stayed at York College, music might not have become the most important thing in my life. I probably would have gone to university and things might have worked out very differently."

There was music in Grimsby. "But it had nearly broken my heart to leave the York choir, where I had sung in the Brahms *Requiem* under Francis Jackson, who had taken over from Edward Bairstow. I remember Ruth Railton, then in charge of the National Youth Orchestra, coming to hear instrumentalists in our school orchestra. She heard a few of us sing, and said that as my voice was breaking, I should not sing for about two years. I was rather devastated by that because I was singing in the church choir and also in a group doing madrigals, but I did exactly as she told me—I never questioned it in my mind. When I began to sing again, in about eighteen months, I found that my voice had fundamentally altered.

"As far as the school was concerned—Wintringham Grammar School— I felt the change very much from the enclosed, small world of York to this big, co-ed school in an industrial town. If I had been there from the start, I should have managed, but coming in as it were in the middle, I simply did not understand the 'language'. It was a jolly good cramming factory and that is not what I wanted."

At the time she left school, the family moved back to York. Janet went to work in a bank and studied music in her spare time at Leeds, also joining the Leeds Philharmonic Choir and singing under Malcolm Sargent. "When the family had to move again because of the demands of my father's job, he realised that I was not going to get all the music I wanted. So I had to choose. Should I go with them or get a transfer from the bank to London and study seriously there? By this time, singing was just beginning to become a more important factor for me. During this last period in York and while I was a member of the Leeds Philharmonic, Allan Wicks—the conductor there— had asked me to take part as a soloist in Haydn's *Nelson Mass*. Ilse Wolf was the soprano soloist. I recall her saying to me that if ever I went to London I should go to Helene Isepp who had taught her. That really put the idea into my mind. If everything worked out and the bank gave me a transfer it wouldn't be an impossibility. Ilse has always been very kind to me and to countless other singers too.

"I could not take such a big step without taking advice from somebody, so I talked to Allan Wicks in a railway carriage soon after that concert and asked him if he thought it was worthwhile me studying music seriously. Like a shot he said, 'Yes, of course I do' and immediately regretted it. I understand exactly how he felt, because I've had to do the same thing myself so often since. To give such direct advice to somebody, which could alter the shape of their lives, is daunting. Who knows, however good the voice may be, how things will turn out? Nobody does. Fortunately I got his split-second reaction and that was enough. I told my mother what he had said and how he had regretted it immediately, and that I was going to go ahead. I simply had to get it out of my system. In any case, my parents said that I could always come home and that it would be an interesting experience whatever happened." That was in 1953.

Already Janet had made her mark locally. In the spring of 1953 at Harrogate, she had been the winner in the Open Class for contraltos in the local music festival. In the Silver Rose Bowl for all voices, she was again the winner. The occasion was noted in *The Yorkshire Post*. A local paper at about the same time praised her performance as soloist in the *Messiah* at Clifton. That *Nelson Mass* was in July 1953, when Ernest Bradbury in *The Yorkshire Post* criticised the fact that Ilse Wolf's name had been in larger type than that

for the rest of the soloists! There were other engagements in the North,
even after she had left for London.

Before going to London, Janet had been to the Edinburgh Festival for her
holiday. She remembers going to a concert given by the Philharmonia
Orchestra and feeling that she really 'belonged' to music. "I knew that I
was part of this life in some very special way. You get those kinds of flashes;
then you go away again and start the kind of life of any music student,
sometimes very hard. It was hard, there is no doubt about it.

"Anyway, the bank was kind. The local head office knew perfectly well
that I was going to leave them as soon as I possibly could. Nonetheless, they
gave me the transfer which, in the circumstances, was a marvellous thing for
them to do. It eased a very, very naïve Yorkshire girl into London. I lived
in a bank hostel in Russell Square where I made friends, which was a great
help in the break from home. I rang up Mrs Isepp and asked 'Can I come and
sing to you?' She had been warned by Ilse and was not unprepared for my
approach. I took lessons with her after banking hours. Because of the huge
amount of work done in a London bank, I was tired out before I got to her;
six months of that was enough. I knew I had to make a decision. I had no
money at all and my parents had not got much either, although they were
doing their best to help. If I left my job they would have to bear the burden
of supporting me for a time.

"One bitterly cold February weekend they came down to talk to Mrs
Isepp. She told them that she could not say whether or not I would have a
wonderful career: it was an impossible thing to predict. She had a hunch that
I would be able to earn my living, but she could not say whether or not I
would have the dedication—and luck—to carry me further. We all decided
that I would take the plunge. I had made up my mind that I was not going
to be a mediocre sort of singer. It had to be all or nothing; otherwise, I would

just sing as a joyful hobby back home where I was longing to be every moment of the day; I was homesick. I do not think I have had all that much of a struggle, but my mother remembers those lonely years of hard work and real misery much better than I do.

"Mrs Isepp never let me practise on my own. After I had left the bank, I went to her two or three times a week. I could not pay for all those lessons so I just gave her what I could. She was really very good to me. I used to practise with Ilse, who not only kept me on an even keel on the days I did not see Helly (Mrs Isepp) but was also a prop in other things. We used to have a meal together or go to the pictures. She made life worth living. The things Ilse Wolf has done for young singers in London could fill a book. With this kind of meticulous overseeing, I managed to conquer my bad vocal habits. I had a good, natural voice and I had not been messed about by anybody. Some people go through terrible experiences with bad teachers, all of which has to be undone. I was able to go ahead because I did what I was told, and I believed in my teacher."

Janet began by learning the general oratorio repertoire because she knew that she would have to begin by earning her money with that. Eventually when Helene Isepp thought she was ready, she told Janet that she could join a choir. Heather Harper, also a pupil of Mrs Isepp, was just leaving the Ambrosian Singers at that time, and she recommended Janet to John Mc-Carthy, conductor of the chorus. "I began to earn a bit, in the Ambrosians and by singing at weddings and funerals. At the same time, I had a part-time job at Morley College as a kind of receptionist—it was three evenings a week and paid my rent. I was at West Square in one half of the College, which was then split in two, and I remember learning *Frauenliebe und Leben* over the fire there."

In the spring of 1955, she had an audition for the BBC and her mother, who has kept a faithful and valuable scrapbook of Janet's early career, still has the letter from the Corporation:

"Dear Miss Baker
We would like to thank you for letting us hear you at a further audition on the 29th of April. This was satisfactory and we hope to be able to offer you a test date in due course. In the meantime, may we emphasise the importance of you sending us, as soon as you can, as complete a list as possible of your current repertoire."

While she was working at Morley College, she was also able to take part in concerts there, singing arias and songs. On July 29th, 1955, she sang for the first time on the radio—gross fee, seven guineas—in a play called *An Island in Time*, produced by Raymond Raikes, music by Anthony Bernard. On October 3rd, she gave her first recital on the BBC, in the Northern Home Service, singing Elgar and Brahms. 'A Music-Lover' wrote her an encouraging note:

"I have just listened to your recital on the Home Service and immediately thought of dear, departed Kathleen Ferrier. What better compliment could be paid to you. Go further, dear lady, go further."

Another letter ran:

"I had to stop my washing machine this morning and listen to your songs. Now that they are finished, I must write to thank you sincerely for the great pleasure they have given me. Your voice reminded me so much of the unspoilt, refreshing charm of Kathleen Ferrier. I can give you no higher praise."

Reviews of her solo performances in such works as the B minor Mass about this time were already noting Janet's warm, compassionate singing.

The Kathleen Ferrier Prize in 1956, then run by the *Daily Mail*, was the next major event in Janet's life. A rather serious car accident in the summer, which had given her bad head injuries, prevented her from entering the London regional stage of the competition. However, she was able to take part in the Northern regional competition at Stockton because her parents came from the district. She won $62.50 as the best of 42 competitors and entered the final on November 30th with 13 other regional winners. At Stockton she sang the 'Inflammatus' from Dvořák's *Stabat Mater*, 'Adieux, forêts' from Tchaikovsky's *Joan of Arc* and Schubert's *Nacht und Träume*. Janet described the finals as "one of the most awful days of one's life". She says that she has always hated the idea of competing with people. "I've always fought against it, because it's a matter of opinion who is the best. Still, that's the way the world works. We have to take exams and go in for competitions.

"I remember I was in the last five in the afternoon and I rang Helly to tell her that as far as I was concerned I was satisfied—I did not want to go any further. Later she told me that, having said that with all sincerity, I deserved to win something. I think all the last five were jolly gifted people and we knew that two were going to be left out."

The first prize, $2500, was won by Barbara Robinson, who has not pursued her career as far as I know. Janet was second and won $1250. *The Daily Telegraph* wrote of her as a "sensitive musician with a voice still undeveloped but of great potential beauty and subtlety." Charles Reid wrote prophetically in *The News Chronicle* that "to my ear the night's most distinguished singing was by second prizewinner, Janet Baker, aged 23, from Stockton-on-Tees, described by the judges as 'a moving and potentially subtle artist'."

And who were those judges—Sir Arthur Bliss, Lord Harewood, Astra Desmond and Joan Cross, who recalled: "The moment I heard Janet sing my whole heart lifted for here was somebody who had a lovely technique as well as a good voice. I remember the Dvořák 'Inflammatus'—I know when a singer is good because cold water goes down my back and it fairly poured down my back while Janet sang this piece. When it came to choose everyone else was for the girl who eventually was given first prize. I said 'As far as I'm concerned there's only one singer here and that's Janet Baker'.

We interviewed three of them. Janet was very sensible and straightforward. She said that she was perfectly happy with her teacher who was doing her no end of good and that she did not want to go off to Italy. Perhaps that went against her. Anyway she only received the second prize. A few years later I met George Harewood at Aldeburgh and he came up to me, saying 'You were right about Janet Baker'."

Lord Harewood recalled that there were two really outstanding singers; "We argued, I remember, about their respective merits. Janet's voice was the smaller, very well contained, very beautiful, very much the timbre it is now in embryo, cool and collected, musically correct and so on. The other girl was a sort of tearaway Amneris, a big, hefty, uninhibited type of singer, and I thought that this was the voice that needed more care from a teacher than Janet's did, and I must say that it's something I have often regretted since. It does not seem to have done much harm—and it does not seem to have done the other lady any good. On the day, though, it was very difficult to choose. I thought my arguments were right, but subsequent events suggest they were wrong."

Janet certainly nurses no hard feelings—quite the reverse. "That was the first time I met Lord Harewood and ever since he has been a factor in my life. I have a very special regard for him because he has always popped up at crucial moments in my life and lent me support. He never talks much to me or says 'that was fantastic', but somehow I feel that he approves. It's terrifying when one knows he is in the audience because he is so knowledgeable. I do appreciate him—specially because he is from Yorkshire. Looking back on that competition again, I feel that perhaps an outstanding talent like the winner's when it's not allied to so many other things really does not get there, while the worker with the lesser talent often does."

While the competition was taking place, Janet was preparing to make what seems to have been her first operatic appearance, in the Oxford University Opera Club's performances of Smetana's *The Secret*. Her role was Roza, and Desmond Shawe-Taylor described it in *Opera* magazine as "the out-

In 'The Secret' at Oxford, 1956.
[*Studio Edmark*

standing performance of the evening", and continued: "She presented a thoroughly credible character, and her singing was unusually true and distinct; so good a voice, together with such taste and feeling for the stage, should take her far." Prophetic words indeed. *The Times* commented: "Miss Baker . . . is certainly a singer of dramatic promise for she delivered her words on a stream of expressive tone from a voice of wide range coloured by a feeling for character". In *The Guardian*, Colin Mason commented; "Oxford did their enthusiastic best for it (the opera), Janet Baker in particular singing with mature professional style and assurance, and with beautifully controlled voice production she made all that could possibly be made of the one principal part in a performance that strongly confirmed her right to her prize in the recent Kathleen Ferrier competition."

That autumn Janet also attended the legendary Lotte Lehmann master classes in London. These helped her in the interpretation of Lieder as Meriel St Clair, to whom Janet had gone with Helene Isepp's blessing, helped her with English and French songs. "Meriel really opened the door for me to French music. She was very sensible, never trying to alter my technique but just helping me in interpretative matters, and also in improving my stage presence. I used to think very hard about what I was singing, but it was not really getting over to the audience. I had not learnt the secret of unlocking what I felt, and I find now that many young singers never seem able to get over this hurdle. Meriel used to say that however hard I was trying I was looking like a lump of pudding. That shocked me terribly. What one has to try to do is make a phrase live without, as it were, 'putting it on'. It is the most difficult thing one has to learn—it is something that has to appear in yourself at a particular moment because of living: it's life that does it. It's the moment that you change from a student and an executant into a performer. The real step is taken by something psychological inside yourself. That was a difficult turning point in my life.

"As far as Lehmann is concerned, I learned from her because she is a special sort of woman. I was coming into contact with a really great performer and of course something rubbed off. We had to come on to the platform of the Wigmore Hall as if we were pleased to see the audience; otherwise she would send us off. I also remember us gathering in the Green Room at the back and being terrified."

At this time, Janet got married. On December 29th, 1956, the *Stockton Gazette* announced the engagement between James Keith Shelley and Janet Baker. "I was going up to Stockton as and when I could afford it. Our families knew each other and we used to play tennis together. I was a very sporty girl and I loved the open-air life. I did not know many people so my mother suggested I might like to play with Keith, who was the son of a friend of hers. He apparently was horrified because he thought I might be a 'rabbit' at the game and would ruin his club reputation. But as soon as I got hold of a racket he knew what I was about. On the first occasion, we managed to beat a couple of members of the tennis team; of course after that I was 'in' and could do no wrong.

"Immediately I was very at home with him and his family. They were the kind of people I knew and had been brought up with, and theirs was the sort of humour I knew, quite apart from Keith's kindliness. I knew that I had never met anybody like that in London. At that time, I suppose he represented to me the North of England. I was 24 and he was 28 so we were not young kids: we knew straight away that there was something important there. But, of course, I went back to London, and we were separated. After my following visit home, we began to write to each other and then he wanted to join me in London. I think his family found the idea strange; they thought I would have to go up there if I was to get engaged to him. Keith had realised—and it was very good of him—that he would have to move to me. I have never thought about it until now, but it was really remarkable of him to have done that, because—who knows—I could have been an absolute failure. We got engaged that Christmas and married the following autumn—we had known each other just over a year. My parents wanted to give us a big wedding, but I hated the thought of it. I said 'give us the money instead', so we got married quietly—and I have regretted it ever since. It's an occasion for one's mother and I did mine out of it. She's had many marvellous occasions since to celebrate, but not that."

With her husband, Keith Shelley.
[Plain Dealer Photo

The Ferrier award and the Lehmann classes gave Janet lots of publicity. After hearing her sing *Frauenliebe und Leben*, Mrs Emmie Tillett, of Ibbs and Tillett, put Janet on their books and began to help her (she has been with the same agents ever since); so, in 1957, Janet really started to get engagements. There were all the stock oratorios up and down the country, and the musical societies. "I also had a marvellous opportunity with the Arts Council at that time. There were Arts Council parties, where representatives from music clubs came to listen to certain artists whom the Council thought they should hear. This was marvellous for me, of course. I remember I went on tour with an oboe player and a pianist. We gave joint recitals, which gave me a chance to find out what people liked to hear. You learned to sing under the worst possible conditions, in awful little rooms where one's voice did not sound well. That really gave me a good background. When people ask me what were the important things at that time, I tell them *those* were the important occasions. They were my life and I could not imagine anything more significant then. I was just doing my job and learning it."

Her name began to appear more and more frequently in the *Radio Times* as she sang more and more for the BBC. She was also beginning to make her mark as a fine Bach singer. At this time, Michael Kennedy wrote in the Northern edition of *The Daily Telegraph* about a *Matthew Passion* performance: "The contralto arias were sung by Janet Baker, who has one of the loveliest true mezzo registers I have heard for some time."

At this juncture Janet was having some difficulty actually running her career. "I was all over the place with my income tax through not writing things down properly. It was a very small mess because I was not earning much at the time but it frightened me, as I recall. I devised a system—and we follow it to this day—which is to put aside a certain sum out of each fee

With Raymond Leppard, who has partnered Janet in the opera house, at recitals and on records. [EMI

so that I knew what was mine, what belongs to my agent, what was going on expenses, and what belonged to the tax man."

Raymond Leppard, who has accompanied her and worked with her on many occasions, remembers it was not only in financial matters that she was then disorganised. "The first time I ever worked with her we were doing the music Purcell wrote for *The Tempest*. She came to rehearse and I thought to myself that this was really going to be something. She was very shy and modest. Then on the morning of the concert when we should have done the final rehearsal, she said she could not come because of another engagement, so I told her that really she could not then do the concert itself."

Since that time her husband, having given up his own work, has become her business manager and she now relies entirely on him to organise her whole life. They have both made a conscious decision not to have children. "People were always bothering me about children. They thought if you got married, you must have children. It seemed for them to be a natural progression. I never could accept that. I have always felt so conscientious about it: I felt that if I had a child then it would have to take first place in my life and that life would be so complicated. How could I leave it? How could I afford a nanny in those early days? The fact is, my career would have to stop and that I could not stand. I know that colleagues of mine have an absolute heartbreak each time they have to leave their children.

" It may seem a difficult thing to admit but my sense of fulfilment has come through my job—I do not feel frustrated at all. I get peculiar letters from people saying that I should have children and that I will regret my decision when the time comes for me to retire. Certainly I felt then, at the end of the fifties, that I could not really afford to take two or three years off. It may be a very selfish attitude to take. In one way it is; in another it is very unselfish because I am not depriving a child of its mother. Keith is of the same mind. If we had a child, we would probably be marvellously happy, and I am sure we would be good parents. People also said marriage needs children. That always seemed an appalling idea: that you needed children to keep you together. It is certainly a wrong reason for having them. I am sure with them our life would have been enriched but one cannot have everything in this world, and we have a terrific life together."

The decision by Keith to give up his own job came when Janet began to get work abroad. "I used to be so lonely. I do not mind being alone and I love reading, but that was beyond reasonable limits. Keith was also lonely, trying to look after himself and being very unselfish about it. One year before leaving for Australia, I discussed the question with the Gerald Moores, who said that we had to make a decision. They saw us beginning to lead separate lives, have our own friends. After much thought, we came to the decision that he would give up his post, and we would make a partnership of it. At first he found it very hard. When he came down the first Monday morning after he had left the office, he sat on a sofa shaking his head, saying 'You know, I've made a terrible mistake.' At first, I was unreasonable, thinking that he should know everything about the musical world, but as time passed, he just took over—whether it was at home, in a plane, or a hotel. He would sit me down in a seat and tell me to get on with reading a score, or whatever, while he dealt with every formality. I began to realise that I would no longer have to fight my way round the world alone. He now loves the life and his knowledge of music has grown from nothing to something very respectable. We simply could not have reckoned on it working out so well: firstly, that his business acumen would be so useful; secondly, that we can stand being together all of the time."

In 1958, she made another operatic appearance, this time at Morley College as Orpheus in Gluck's opera, produced by Joan Cross (John Copley, now a Covent Garden producer, did the choreography). Peter Gellhorn was the conductor. Miss Cross remembers Janet had made such an impression on her at the Ferrier competition that she was very happy to be working with Janet on a production.

The producer, Anthony Besch, first worked with Janet in the Glyndebourne Chorus in 1956. "That year she was part of the off-stage chorus in *Idomeneo*. I had to hand out the palms to the singers. Carl Ebert used to tell us who was to have and who was not to have these and I wrote down their names. Janet was one of those *with* a palm. I was hardly aware of her as a

Top: Centre, as the Second Witch in the Ingestre production of 'Dido and Aeneas'. [Guy Gravett

Above: As Eduige in the Handel Opera Society's production of 'Rodelinda' with Joan Sutherland in the title role. [Houston Rogers

personality then, of course, but the following year we started a small opera festival at Ingestre, the home then of Lord and Lady Shrewsbury. I was director of productions, and in the first year we did *Dido and Aeneas* as part of a double-bill. We had a mainly Glyndebourne contingent. Moran Caplat had heard Janet at the Ferrier competition and told me I must take notice of her marvellous voice, so we gave her the part of the Second Witch. One immediately noticed that she was a singer of great intensity and completely identified with her role. As a Yorkshire girl, she had the kind of cool diffidence I associate with people from that county—they do not accept you until they really get to know you. Nothing was taken for granted in her work either; she would always weigh up things and think them out with the greatest care. Indeed, to this day, she requires to work out everything completely to her own satisfaction, which is very refreshing.

"The following year we went elsewhere with the festival and used another cast. Then in 1959, the production of *Dido* went to Bath. Joan Hammond was Dido, Heather Harper took Belinda, and Janet progressed to the part of the Sorceress. Colin Davis, the conductor, introduced a lot of embellishments, and I think Janet coped with them better than any other member of the cast. Then we took it to the Banqueting Hall at Hampton Court, a wonderful experience as one imagined these were the kind of surroundings *Dido* was performed in to begin with."

The Times wrote of this performance; "The vocal honours of the performance went to Miss Janet Baker, as the Sorceress, an impressive and flexible voice finely handled." That year she won the Queen's Prize worth $375

Also in 1959, Janet sang in Paul Steinitz's annual performance of Bach's

Matthew Passion, which then took place in St Bartholomew's Church in the City of London. Desmond Shawe-Taylor in *The Sunday Times* praised Janet's singing. "She sang the most important contralto arias smoothly and expressively without a hint of the plumminess that afflicts so many oratorio contraltos". Since that time Janet has done her best to take part in each year's account, and also if possible in one at least of the Bach Choir's performances of this work. Every time she sings the alto arias she seems to breathe more life into them.

In October of that year, she made her only appearance to date at the Wexford Festival—as Pippo in Rossini's *Gazza Ladra*. Shawe-Taylor was again lavish in his praise: "Miss Baker's spontaneous charm and clear singing made something quite memorable of the scene in which Nanetta visits Pippo in prison."

Her prowess as a Handel singer, in works other than the *Messiah*, really dates from her performances with the Handel Opera Society in *Rodelinda* in 1959. Joan Sutherland sang the title role; Janet Baker was Eduige. Anthony Besch was the producer. Andrew Porter wrote in *Opera*: "Janet Baker (Eduige) is one of the most arresting, intelligent and imaginative mezzos we have, with vivid declamation and a rich, ringing, individual timbre." She appeared again with the H.O.S. in 1962 as Storge in *Jephtha*; the same critic wrote that her role was "beautifully sung, passionately interpreted".

As Dido in Purcell's opera at Glyndebourne in 1966. [Guy Gravett

Anthony Besch, who was again the producer, remembers her marvellous performance of Storge's dramatic aria about her nightmare: "One was beginning to identify her with these very dramatic parts. They were not necessarily heavy for singing, but it was the kind of drama and intensity she could inject into them."

In the meantime, she had begun her long and fruitful association with Sir Anthony Lewis, then at the Barber Institute in Birmingham, now Principal of the Royal Academy of Music in London. He first asked her to sing Dido (a further promotion) in *Dido and Aeneas*, the first time she had sung the part. That was in 1961. Janet said: "I thought it was a strange thing for him to ask me to do. He explained that he thought it should have the character of a dark voice. And it was true that, although I had been trained as an alto, I had the higher range. People said my voice had gone up, but that is not so; the notes were always there but they were not being used. So when I came to sing Dido and the Handel *travesti* roles, my equipment was ready to cope with them."

Sir Anthony Lewis had heard Janet first in the *Dido and Aeneas* at Hampton Court and he was immediately struck by the beauty of her voice and her very stylish way of singing. It was directly as a result of this that, when Oiseau-Lyre decided to record *Dido*, under Lewis, an invitation was extended to her to take the title role. He believes that that performance revealed a new singer of exceptional quality. "It was the beginning of a very close partnership."

He had begun his series of Handel productions in 1959 at the Barber Institute. "When we reached *Tamerlano* in 1962, Janet was obviously one of the artists we thought of. She took the role of Irene, not a principal role, but she made it into one. In one of the arias she sang, Handel introduces clarinets for the first time into the theatre, and she was so struck with the piece that she decided to sing it at a Prom. And when she came to take her honorary Doctorate of Music at Birmingham, I suggested to the Vice Chancellor that instead of making the usual speech of acceptance at the ceremony, she should reply in kind—and she sang this aria again, much to the delight of those present." Of the Birmingham performance, the Handel scholar Winton Dean wrote in *Opera*: "Janet Baker's Irene was quite exquisite, both musically and dramatically, with firm tone, beautiful line and a perfect stage presence."

From that time until the performances in Birmingham came to an end with Lewis's move to London, Janet appeared in most productions. "She was unable to be with us for *Xerxes* the following year but she returned to us for the title role in *Ariodante* in 1964 and for Rameau's *Hippolyte et Arice* in 1965, which we recorded, and also took to the Oxford Bach Festival. Then she sang the title role in *Orlando* in 1966—which we brought to Sadler's Wells. Finally she returned for *Admeto* in 1968, in which she sang Alcestis.

"The characteristic that comes through all her work and gives such distinction to whatever she sings is a feeling of being involved. This comes right out from her. One speaks of actors being inside their parts and this, I think, can be applied to Janet without any qualification; she has completely absorbed every part she tackles and this emerges in her singing. One of her great virtues as a Handel singer, apart from her innate sense of style, is that she understands not only his broad characterisation of a role but his individual characterisation of arias. This is quite vital for a Handel singer because it is within this kind of characterisation that Handel makes his most important contribution to the drama. Having studied each very closely, Janet will have a very clear idea about their nature. That immediately places her in a category of her own.

"She also has the right tempo of movement for a Handel opera. She has superb self-control, and she is therefore not at all worried by the comparatively slow pace with which the dramatic thread is unravelled in a Handel aria. Then, of course, she has a natural dignity. But, in an 18th-century *opera seria*, it is the vocal line that is the main vehicle of the drama; so the subtlety of inflection and variety of sound and meaning she brings to her singing are ideal—she never sings a meaningless musical phrase. Working with Janet on ornamentation is a fascinating process; it is just the way they should evolve. We look at the role together; I put forward suggestions for decoration, cadenzas and so on, bearing in mind the style of each aria and her particular vocal quality; she tries these out and comes back with counter-proposals; then we come to decisions. And everything becomes so integrated with the original aria that it seems naturally part of it. There is never anything extraneous about Janet's ornaments; they come out of the music, which is exactly how it should be.

"She will always arrive, putting the rest of the cast to shame, with her

As Handel's Ariodante at the Barber Institute, Birmingham, in 1964. [Reilly and Constantine

part fully memorised. She has a fantastic memory and I do not think I remember her ever faltering. She is also quite rigorous in knowing the extent of her own capabilities, and will never take on a role beyond them.

"She also has the quality of radiance possessed by Kathleen Ferrier. That comes through in her singing, this wonderful inner harmony. There is communication all the time, too. I remember when we began our series of performances, the Handelian conventions were not as readily accepted as they are today—she had to overcome a doubting reaction from the audience. However, as soon as she stepped on the stage, whatever may have gone before in the way of unintentional amusement on the part of the audience, she could re-establish the serious nature of the work. She obviously believes in what she is doing and so she carries her audience with her. Off the stage, she relaxes completely."

Stanley Sadie corroborated Sir Anthony's evidence in his review in *Opera* of *Ariodante* in 1964: "One is apt to feel a slight touch of superiority when reading those 18th-century writers on opera who seem to care about nothing but singing: we, of course, mind about Higher Things, like the relationship of music to drama. But I came away from the Barber Institute

ready to join their number. Hearing Janet Baker in Ariodante's arias made
me very much aware how vitally important the quality of singing really is
in a Handel opera. We tend nowadays to assume that the notion that his
operas are monstrously hard to sing is not true, simply because there are
plenty of singers who can get round the notes, but there is a difference
between getting round the notes and getting really into them, as Miss Baker
illustrated: a strikingly powerful musical personality such as hers reveals a
new dimension to the music. This is surely just what the contemporary
audiences admired so much in the great singers of their time. Miss Baker
is of this class—a voice of great depth and beauty, an ability to identify herself utterly with the emotions she is called upon to express, and a technique
which enables her to sing Handel's semiquaver runs with power and clarity
as well as to rise to top Gs and As, with a gentle *mezza voce* over virtually
her whole compass."

The other important development in Janet's career at the beginning of the
1960s was her connection with Benjamin Britten and the English Opera
Group. Early in 1962, she received a letter from Peter Pears, asking if she
had ever sung Dido. "Don't you think you could and should? Send me a
postcard with 'Yes' on it and I will tell Ben Britten. Please." She accepted
and was told that there was a probability of performances in Sweden as well
as at Aldeburgh. In fact, the former took place first—in May at Drottningholm. The connection between the E.O.G. and Covent Garden had just
begun, and Keith Grant had been taken on as manager. "Some five weeks
after I'd joined this organisation, I had to take the English Opera Group and
Benjamin Britten with it to Drottningholm. This was something of a
baptism of fire. Janet was one of about the first half dozen singers I got to
know and I vividly remember how easy-going and helpful she was, hard

working and professional too. Speaking as a manager of artists, I can say that I wish they were all like her. I think she was quite nervous about those performances because they were quite important for her. I could not imagine a more beautiful impersonation of the part. The simplicity of her approach was particularly memorable. She was concentrating terribly hard because she found the task quite awesome, especially as Ben had done his own realisation of it and was conducting the work himself. The performances at Aldeburgh were in the Jubilee Hall, not perhaps such an ideal setting as Drottningholm, but there we had the benefit of the English Chamber Orchestra, which was a great help."

Peter Stadlen in *The Daily Telegraph* shared Keith Grant's view of Janet's Dido. "Janet Baker humanised Dido and projected the impression of doomed love from the very beginning", and Colin Mason in *The Guardian* commented: "Janet Baker's every phrase and inflection is deeply moving from the tormented languish of her first scene to the startling light and serene 'Remember me' of her last." John Warrack wrote in *Opera*: "Janet Baker, once an impressive Sorceress, has now successfully graduated to Dido—a performance of real tragic strength. She reserved the 'pathetic' inflections in the voice for a few well-placed strokes such as the fining away of tone to a ghostly *piano* at 'Remember me', making her dramatic points more by her understanding of the dignity and sense of direction in Purcell's melodic line."

At Aldeburgh, 1969.

Janet remembers her own feelings at that time. "I have always been lucky in so many ways. I have never been what is normally thought of as ambitious, in the sense that I wanted to do this, that and the other in various places— I have never had performing goals other than wanting to just sing whatever came my way as well as I could. This still applies today. I like things to come naturally to me. They certainly did in respect of opening out a new repertoire at about this period."

What was Britten's influence? "I think, above all, it was his high performing standards. You went to Aldeburgh in fear and trembling, knowing that if you passed muster, it would set a seal on your work. His opinion of me and the way he works has a unique significance in this country. My first experience with the Festival was singing Lennox Berkeley's *Poems of St Teresa* in Blythburgh Church—I suppose that must have been in 1961, and after that I joined the E.O.G. I have worked with the Group ever since. It was a great eye-opener to be in that environment.

"Britten has a strange effect on people. It is like being drawn by a magnet to this fantastic personality. When one is very young it can be an all-possessing experience. When you are with him, you feel that there's nobody else except Benjamin Britten. Even now I feel it, after knowing him all these years. One has to be careful or he will quite dominate your life and your thinking. Because of this quality, and the great respect one has for him as one of the great human beings of our time, and as a musician—once you have done a work with him, you feel you cannot do it with anybody else. You emerge from the experience as though you had never performed it before.

Now, when I return to Aldeburgh, it is like going home—this is the source to which one returns at intervals in order to be put right, renewed, but I have to go away again to bring back to Aldeburgh experiences that I have had as an artist. Most of us have a tremendous love for him and for his work and for what he has done for us all these years. It is a very special thing— but still frightening. I am sure he does not realise that because he is always so happy to see you and so grateful for whatever you do. And Peter, too. One cannot begin to describe what an effect they have on musical life."

Two of Janet's next roles with the E.O.G. were Polly Peachum in Britten's realisation of *The Beggar's Opera* and Nancy in *Albert Herring*. Those who 'discovered' Janet as a comedian in *Così fan tutte* are apt to forget that she had already done these parts earlier in her career. These were productions by Colin Graham, whom Janet has always liked to work with as a producer. Keith Grant comments that this showed another side to her altogether. "Whenever we do the work again, I still remember her as Polly—her sense of humour and her fine treatment of the dialogue. I do not think Nancy was one of her best parts, although she sang it beautifully. Nancy is a flirtatious piece, and Janet is not that.

"1964 was the year of the Group's great Russian tour on which Janet sang Lucretia for the first time. We did 29 performances in 32 days in three different cities with a company of 34, a real endurance test for all concerned. Janet had done Polly in Edinburgh when we were alternating *The Beggar's Opera* with Colin Graham's new production of *The Rape of Lucretia* at the Festival. It was because we had such a small company that everyone had to have at least two roles in their repertory, and Janet, in fact, learned Nancy for the tour.

"As far as I recall Ben was not too keen for her to take Lucretia on in the first place. He felt that it was going to be too low for her. I mean he loves her to do anything—but I think he was worried for her sake. He was still dubious after she had first begun to sing it, but as time went on she swept away any doubts he may have had.

"I was bothered least by Janet, even though the tour was a gruelling one. She always looked after herself, and did not cause any difficulties. We had eighteen people ill at one time, and only just managed to keep the curtain up. Janet got ill in Moscow, on the last leg of the tour, and she was whisked off to hospital. The bass David Kelly visited her and saw that she was very worried. He got hold of me, and with the help of the British embassy we had her flown back to England.

"She has matured greatly in the role of Lucretia, and I think the performances in the Maltings in 1970 were the distillation of all that is best in the E.O.G. Any difficulties she had when she first sang the part have been completely overcome, and the role now sits quite comfortably in her voice. As an interpretation, she first approached Lucretia very gingerly. She did not then have the sophisticated dramatic technique to bring it off fully. She was a slightly nervous, rather than an authoritative Lucretia. Now she has this extraordinary dignity and poise which she at first had difficulty in achieving."

Lord Harewood is also of the opinion that something happened to transform Janet's performances during the mid-1960s. "For the first few years of Janet's blossoming career, I used to think there was a rather inhibited quality to her singing, which one could put down to a rather English want not to wear your heart on your sleeve. That used to worry me. The beauty of the voice, the musicianship and all that was never in question. The sound was perfectly made and unstrained. When or why that inhibition went, I am not sure, because of course it did go completely. I think her voice grew and her confidence grew with it, and she then felt that she would not harm it if she allowed herself a bit looser rein—it may have been something that happened unconsciously, instinctively.

"One likes to think that learning a particular role or working with a particular person opened doors for her; perhaps it did, but certainly some time in the middle sixties, one realised that the beautiful and to-be-admired artist had become something much bigger than that. What I now found especially valuable and remarkable was her ability to suggest a kind of stillness and repose which singers who have always been able to convey drama and excitement—the more violent emotions—have never had and will probably never have. It is the most difficult thing to create. Janet can manage this serenity in her singing, it seems to me, easily, because she does it so well and so often. That was true of her Lucretia. Since then, she has added enormously to her range, not least with Scottish Opera—comedy as Dorabella in *Così fan tutte* and emotional power as Dido in *The Trojans*. These assumptions only go to confirm the idea that we should ask our singers to extend their range. Now I would like her to look at the big Rossini roles."

As Lucretia in Britten's opera.

While Janet's operatic career was developing, she was also coming on apace as a concert singer. By 1960, her Lieder were apparently already beginning to make their mark. The actor Richard Bebb, also an authority on singing, wrote to her in August of that year: "What very great joy your Wolf recital gave me tonight. Several of the songs I have never heard better versions of. In some very wonderful way, you seem to have captured the great secrets of Elena Gerhardt and Lotte Lehmann—Gerhardt's line and feeling and overall atmosphere, and Lotte's marvellous impulsiveness. May I also say that of its type your voice seems to be the very best we have had since Kerstin Thorborg. Much power to your arm and be assured that quietly you are gaining for yourself a very considerable body of admirers." There were many other letters also praising that and several subsequent broadcast recitals.

Janet made her Prom début in the 1960 season, singing Sosostris's aria from Tippett's *The Midsummer Marriage*. She had sung that role in a famous broadcast performance of the opera, conducted by Norman Del Mar, in the same year. *The Daily Telegraph* commented on the Prom performance that she entered into the role: "wholeheartedly with her deep, seductive tone and sustained intensity of phrasing." The same paper described her as "A Bach singer in a hundred" for her performance in the *Matthew Passion* under

Cutting the 21st birthday cake of the London Bach Society. Paul Steinitz, the Society's musical director is on the right.

Paul Steinitz that year. The same year and in 1961 she had begun to sing Mahler—the Second Symphony under Klemperer and *Lieder eines fahrenden Gesellen* at Morley College—and Elgar—the Angel in *The Dream of Gerontius.*

She was becoming much better-known as she gave recitals and appeared in concerts all over the country. In 1964, to commemorate the tenth anniversary of the Kathleen Ferrier award, she was chosen to give a recital at the Wigmore Hall. Andrew Porter wrote in *The Financial Times*: "There would be little dispute that of all British singers, Janet Baker has the most beautiful voice or that she uses this voice, a mezzo-soprano that reaches easily in the soprano and contralto range, with taste, intelligence and innate musicianship. Miss Baker pursues a mixed career, dividing her time between the theatre, concert hall, and Lieder platform. I find her most impressive of all in the theatre; challenging roles such as Handel's Ariodante which makes exorbitant demands on technique, stamina and temperament, brings out all that is almost remarkable in her. Purcell's Dido touches in her a note of passionate expressiveness and the most vivid moments of her Wigmore Hall recital occurred in the only operatic aria in the programme, 'Parto, parto' from Mozart's *La Clemenza di Tito*."

In the summer of 1964 she gave one of the vocal recitals in Goldsmith's Hall as part of that year's City of London Festival and was again much praised. And she closed the Hallé's 1964 season singing the alto part in Mahler's Second Symphony, under Barbirolli's direction. At this time, he was an important influence on her career. Janet remembers how they began to collaborate. "I made a test tape for him and he said that he wanted me quite definitely as the Angel in his recording of *Gerontius*. This was a big step for him to take because of Kathleen. For a long time, any mezzo was non-existent to him. He had to use other mezzos and he was a kind man, who would never say that you were not reaching her standards. But I felt it desperately at first. He judged us all by her and it was grievous for him to hear the same music sung by anyone else. He would get out Kathleen's last letter to him and become awfully upset. I worked with him under these circumstances for some time. Then, quite suddenly, he began to take me on my own terms. That was marvellous.

"He was an emotional man—his music was from the heart. That is what I liked about him. One might not agree with everything he did, but there was this true human being with a lot of love in him; it was all-embracing, and irresistible musically because he would stand there and you could tell how much he was feeling from the expression on his face. He would communicate to you this affection he had for the phrase, and you caught that love as well even in pieces like Elgar's *Sea Pictures*. It is not my favourite work by any means, but it's really one of my favourite recordings. Our *Nuits d'été* together are perhaps at the wrong speeds but nevertheless . . . there is something about them and that is John."

Rehearsing with Sir John Barbirolli. [EMI

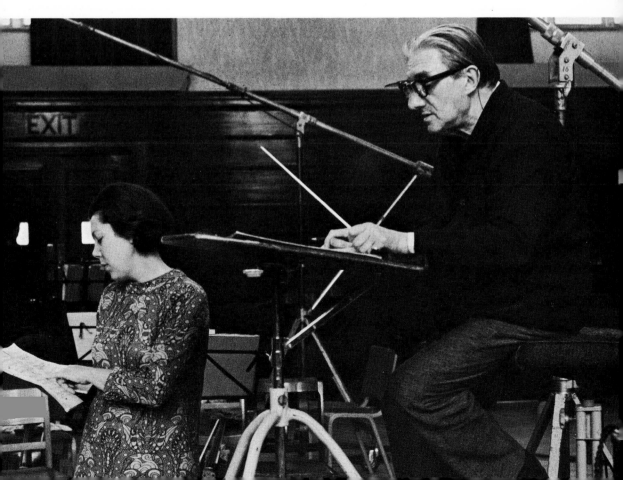

Janet believes that she absorbs something from everyone she has worked with. "I am like blotting paper in that respect. You can learn from anybody you work with or just talk to. I recall Klemperer. Heather Harper and I had to go and sing for him—the *Midsummer Night's Dream* solos, I think. I was terrified. Heather was awfully good with him right from the start—she is such a natural, confident person—and she could deal with him. I never could joke with him as she could. She gave as good as she got, which was just the right way to cope. It took me years to do that. Since that time, I have had marvellous musical experiences working with him in Beethoven and Mahler. He is a great man. If you are sitting in a room with a person like that, with all those years of experience behind him, it enriches one's life. You come away from a series of performances with him and others like him a different person. George Szell was another who had the gift of triggering off something inside you."

Janet gave a great number of recitals on the BBC at this time, in the mid-sixties, concentrating very much on unhackneyed Schubert songs. "So many singers can be heard doing the well-known Schubert, and I feel it is my duty as a more mature performer to introduce to the public things which a younger singer might not be able to manage, because they have not the same selling power. I do not mean to be presumptuous—I just mean that audiences will take something from me that they would not from a beginner. I love doing the famous ones—famous because they are probably the best—but there are other, very interesting facets of his music that need to be heard.

"My range helps. I am not tied to a certain tessitura so I can tackle things that are a bit far out in that way. I do not mind if there is the occasional

Recording 'Nuits d'été' with Sir John Barbirolli. [EMI

high or low note because I can reach them. The same is true of operatic parts."

Gerald Moore has been of great assistance to her in this field; and she gave several recitals with him as accompanist just before he retired from public performance, apart from the records they have made together. "I very much regret that we did not have a longer public association. I love him dearly and in the studio he is an enormous help to me, and suggests things for me as though he had never played for any other Lieder singer. He has this marvellous ability himself to put the whole picture of the song into his introduction; there is the scene set for you, and you just come in and carry on. His support is such that he leaves you free to do what you like on top. Unless you are a performer, you just cannot know what he gives. So the records we have done together are very precious to me."

Gerald Moore himself recalled an occasion twelve years ago when he was rehearsing with Dietrich Fischer-Dieskau. "During a break he asked me if I had accompanied anybody interesting lately, and I replied that I had been playing for the first London recital of Janet Baker. He said he had never heard of her. I said that I thought he would—very soon. We recorded that evening and the next day we were rehearsing again, and he told me that he had heard Janet in the meantime. 'I tuned into some broadcast from England. She was singing with a conductor and orchestra who were not very good, but she is marvellous. I doubt if there is anyone on the Continent here who can approach her'. Since then they have become great friends."

Moore believes that she has one endowment shared by very few artists. "She is able to put an audience completely at their ease, because she seems

Working with Gerald Moore on a Schubert song. [EMI

With Jacqueline du Pré and Daniel Barenboim in New York.

to be unaware of technical difficulties. Now I think that this is a quality shared with Elisabeth Schumann and Fischer-Dieskau. They all seem able to sing just for the sheer joy of it. That almost suggests they do not have to work or prepare, but they sing with perfect ease and the work starts from there onwards. It does not mean that they do not have nerves but they go on the stage with the assurance that all will be well.

"Janet is very conscientious and she is a quick 'study', a hard worker, and extremely self-critical. To me she is charming and modest; she is 'Janet' for whom everybody feels warmth and affection. She welcomes criticisms and suggestions, perhaps inspiration. She is never content to follow the usual rut in matters of repertoire, and she is constantly expanding it in both the German and French fields. She once brought me a song of Schubert that till then I had never played—*Gondelfahrer*. She does not want to record easy successes with established chestnuts.

"From the accompanist's point of view, the most important attribute for an artist is that she or he should be a good musician like Janet. She has a good idea of the structure of each song. There must be a navigational plan: and then that can be discussed. Within that framework you can make spontaneous adjustments. That is what Janet does. Although she is so English in many ways, restrained in her manner, she is tremendously full-blooded at the climax of a song, or when it comes to sensing the innermost feeling of a song. Sometimes she will do something unexpected, something brought about by the inspiration of the moment. If you have a rapport—as we have—the accompanist can anticipate that and go along with the singer."

Raymond Leppard, who has also accompanied Janet on many occasions, feels much the same way. "It is the excitement of the actual performance. She is not altogether predictable. What you do is based on rehearsal but it *is* a performance every time, not the exact reproduction of what you have rehearsed. The whole thing with her can suddenly take off, and it is a wonderful feeling when it does, quite extraordinary; tremendous intensity comes out of it, catching you up in the mood of the song.

"She also has a retentive memory for corrections, which is something rare to find in singers. Even though she has learnt a mistake and it has found its way into a production rehearsal, you tell her that it is an E not an F, and it is there for good as a correction. She also has this extraordinary equanimity. When she is working, she works really hard—lots of laughs, but it is real concentration all the time. There is a marvellous sense of questing for what there is to be got out of the music in hand, its significance. She has also improved out of all recognition, profiting from every experience. This enriches all she does. That will go on—and I am sure she is one of those singers who will be worth hearing when she is seventy. It is this expressive power that is in the voice. I noticed it the very first time I heard her. Many other voices may be very beautiful but it is always the same sound. She dares to do things others would not attempt."

The period between 1966 and 1968 saw the biggest leap ahead in Janet's career. In the autumn of 1966 she made her New York début as a recitalist.

The New York Times reported: "Last night she wrapped a Town Hall audience round her little finger in her first New York recital. She can do about anything vocally and dramatically in a variety of contexts and she does it all with a communicative radiance and personal warmth that border on magic. The French songs were the high point of the programme: for these her projection of style and content were unrivalled by any present-day singer. The large audience, which included many singers and musicians, hung on every word. In short, this was a début to remember."

The World-Journal Tribune wrote: "Recitalists like Janet Baker are so rare that her début last night became one of the events of the season. Her audience sat entranced and left reluctantly after several encores. Here is a singer who warms the soul. Endowed with a beautifully rounded mezzo-soprano, she sings with a purity of tone, a keen sense of style, an impeccable taste. As song followed song, the wonder grew that she sustained her artistry on such a high plane. Spontaneous bravos came as she finished her second number. The experience grew richer as the recital advanced. The Fauré songs were sheer joy as she sang them so refreshingly. This was a memorable début recital: Miss Baker should crowd the concert halls from now on."

That she has done as much in America, on several tours, as elsewhere, but she has not sung in opera in the U.S., and it is in opera that she advanced so avidly during the succeeding years. "My image, if I must use that word, until this time had not been as an opera singer, and yet from my point of view every single year of my working life I have done a role on stage, which means that I have developed, I think, in the right way, not shutting out any experience. You cannot shut out Lieder, or the great experience of singing Bach; you cannot shut out opera either. You have to be as serious about, and absorbed in, every aspect of performing life; otherwise you are maimed in some way. So it makes me mad when someone says that I have only been doing opera recently. I have only been doing opera that has hit the public imagination of late, but I have been an opera singer all along. I adore the stage and I think I am a good actress. Frank Dunlop, one of the directors of the National Theatre, told me that I could learn my living as an actress. That is one of the nicest things anybody had ever said to me. I bring it out at every opportunity. And that was after my early Handel operas in Birmingham."

Still, it was with Scottish Opera that Janet's operatic career really took wing. Anthony Besch, the producer, decided he wanted Janet to play Dorabella in his 1967 *Così fan tutte* for that company. "After it had all taken place, Anthony told me that people had been astounded that he had thought of casting the supposedly serious Miss Baker in a comic role. He knew me better, knew that I have got a sense of humour—I am not serious for very long. Anyway, I thought it was a super idea so up we went to Scotland. Elizabeth Harwood, always a dear friend, was to be Fiordiligi. It was an outstanding production; and an occasion in all our lives, in particular in mine because people said 'Oh, Miss Baker can laugh'. I enjoyed the role especially from the acting point of view. As a result of these performances,

Top: As Dorabella, with Elizabeth Harwood as Fiordiligi, in Scottish Opera's production of 'Così fan tutte'. [Bryan & Shear Ltd

Above: 'Così fan tutte' again. [Bryan & Shear Ltd

I had a lot of offers to sing Dorabella abroad but I have tried to contain my operatic career to this country." Harold Rosenthal in *Opera* described this interpertation thus: "as perfect a Dorabella as one could wish for, displaying an unsuspected sense of fun, and singing her arias and duets with a Mediterranean warmth."

Scottish Opera then invited Janet back to sing Dido in their production of the complete *Trojans* of Berlioz in 1969. Janet had sung the Garden Scene from the second part to critical acclaim at a concert to mark the closing of the National Opera School in 1963, so the part was not entirely new to her. She also sang Cassandra at a complete performance with Colin Davis. She thinks that, to date, Dido is the most satisfying part she has sung on stage. "The whole production had an aura of magic about it. It really caught the imagination of the audiences. That finally dispelled the idea that I was just an oratorio and concert performer. There was a new Baker image."

Illness nearly prevented her taking part in the performance. "I think it all stemmed from my tonsils which I now had out (many colleagues have since told me I was crazy to let a surgeon get at my throat). Twenty-four hours before the first night my temperature went up to 103. A doctor gave me antibiotics and I slept for about 16 hours. That brought my temperature down a bit but left me terribly weak and the doctor said I could never go on, but I told him I would do the performance whatever happened; so he gave me drugs and, truthfully, I forgot everything—I did not feel ill at all. Of course, I suffered for it during the next few days and, thank goodness, the next performance was not for another week."

As Dido in Scottish Opera's production of 'The Trojans', 1969.

I myself remember that the occasion was charged with excitement and

I wrote in *The Financial Times*: "Miss Baker's Dido was, as we expected, an in-the-round portrayal, as surely conceived as executed. It is an assumption to treasure along with her other Dido, her Handelian heroines. As passionate in love as she was distraught in desertion—her regal bearing destroyed by Aeneas's betrayal—her acting left nothing to be desired. By a slow turn of the head, a movement of the eye, Miss Baker revealed Dido's burgeoning desire while she used her whole expressive body to depict the enraged queen. In short, a performance of Virgilian proportions. Vocally, she projected the text with unaffected directness matched to a burnished, intense tone. Sometimes she pressed her voice just beyond what nature intended it for, particularly in the penultimate scene—but that may be appropriate for the doomed lover beside herself."

In September that same year, Janet gallantly stepped in for an ailing Josephine Veasey in the Covent Garden production of the same work, although she was already singing Lucretia with the E.O.G. at Sadler's Wells, but it was not quite the same thing as the Glasgow performances because she had not prepared for it. It was not her Covent Garden début; that had taken place back in 1966, when she sang Hermia in Britten's *A Midsummer Night's Dream*. She sang Dido in *The Trojans* again at the Edinburgh Festival and at Covent Garden with great success in the autumn of 1972.

Her next appearance with Scottish Opera was as Octavian in Besch's production of *Der Rosenkavalier* in 1971. "My idea of the role is different from the way one is encouraged to think of the character. He struck me as deadly serious, a real person—that is what I think about all the parts I

The final scene of 'The Trojans'.

portray. My Dorabella is not a slight, flirty girl. She is as much of a person in her own right as Fiordiligi, with a dry, witty approach to life. She only pretends to be a fool. And Octavian is not a young man who will go from love affair to love affair. He may not stay for ever with Sophie, but at the time when the Marschallin tells him that they will part because the world is like that, this is the most appalling tragedy for him; she is making him grow up in five minutes. He understands for the first time what this particular facet of his life is about; it is a revelation—and shattering at that. He must feel this deeply, because he is so hurt by the words that she has spoken, the door is open for his next experience in life.

"Dramatically, it is a very hard role to play. If there is such a doubt in my mind, I go back to the music; the clue is there. You cannot feel something trite when some superb phrase is being played in the orchestra. So my approach to Octavian was, in one sense, very naïve, and so my Octavian is *my* Octavian and not one that is grown out of an operatic tradition, with somebody else's ideas being fed into me. I should love to sing the Composer in *Ariadne* now."

Anthony Besch has a theory that singers who come from Yorkshire have a very strong, inbred musicality and cites Janet, Elizabeth Harwood, Peter Glossop and Joyce Blackham, as very good illustrations. He also believes that they have a very strong theatrical sense. "They have a very particular sense of humour too. That came out when Janet and Elizabeth played together in *Così*; their sense of humour dovetailed one with another. The particular delicacy of their comedy was quite remarkable. There is another thing about Yorkshire people—they do not take anything for granted.

"I remember Janet coming to me during the first run of *Così* and asking how I had ever thought of her for the part of Dorabella. It was really Alexander Gibson's initiative, although naturally we discussed the idea together. We thought that we had never seen her in comedy but her own personality has such an infectious humour—and she has such an impishness about her—that we felt sure to canalise that into a comic role. And our point was in the event proved: she did this kind of high comedy exquisitely.

"Then we came to *Rosenkavalier*—remember three years had intervened and Janet had developed a great deal in the meantime. Elizabeth Harwood, our Sophie, could respond naturally to what I wanted, because she is a born stage person and you have only got to suggest something to her and it is immediately translated into fact, if it is appropriate to her. If not, we all think of something else. Now Janet is not like that. She takes longer to get to the point: it is not that she is slow or holds you up, but she must think very hard about what she is doing. You find as you go through the opera that she is enormously attentive and writes all your points down. Then she goes away, turns over the ideas in her mind, and comes back for the next rehearsal having completely mastered what you have asked her to do.

"Then, with Octavian, there is the *travesti* problem. When some singers are dressed up as young men, you never for a moment forget that they are actually women, even if their figures are right. But Janet reminded me of the occasion when Ronald Pickup played Rosalind at the National Theatre. You cease to think—is this a man or is this a woman? With Janet's Octavian, I felt that she identified herself with the role so much that you did not say to yourself that this was a woman playing Octavian. It was a phenomenon. She took very great care over her wig, dress and makeup. When we said she should wear a chest-flattener, she agreed: indeed she said that we should give it her as soon as possible, so that she could begin to think of herself as a man. That made her stand differently too.

"She was most moving with Helga Dernesch in the final scene of the first act—with Janet, one waits for these serious bits because one knows what she is going to make of them. Then, as Mariandl in the third act, she was hilarious because she under-played the comedy so cleverly. One critic commented that she played it as though Octavian himself was rather afraid of what was going to be the outcome of this flirtation with Ochs."

In February 1968, Janet sang in a concert performance of Gluck's *Orfeo* in San Francisco and a local paper was as enthusiastic about this dramatic portrayal as other Americans about her recital performances. "Janet Baker, despite the excellence of everyone else, stood out all alone. As Orfeo, the greatest singer the world has ever known, she poured out passionate utterance, her face twisted with pain. If anyone else tried an emotion like that I am afraid I would leave the theatre, but Miss Baker is so true to the mark, her passion is so beautifully controlled in her smooth, even voice, that I was simply rooted to my seat, my mouth open, my eyes full of tears. From her first anguished entrance throughout the wide range of exquisite pianissimo, she had the audience in her palm."

Perhaps David Cairns, in the *New Statesman*, summed up her operatic

As Octavian with Helga Dernesch as the Marschallin in Act I of Scottish Opera's production of 'Der Rosenkavalier'. [Bob Anderson

CBE day, 1970, with her mother and husband. [Feature Press

Raymond Leppard, Janet and Peter Hall "plotting" 'La Calisto'. [Glyndebourne

achievement in *Così* and *The Trojans* most cogently when he wrote: "Her interpretation of Dido and Dorabella would alone have justified the creation of Scottish Opera. Beauty of tone, impeccable clarity of diction, a noble style, phrasing at once full-blooded and refined—these could have been foreseen but not such range and power of declamation, such a heady blend of the regal and the womanly, such a sense of the moment when interest quickens into passion, such fine play of eye and gesture, almost anything but this extraordinary flair for the stage. Her performance in *Così* is predictably well sung, but the wit and panache and mastery of timing amount to a revelation as seen through the no less touching and admirable Fiordiligi of Elizabeth Harwood."

Of her Octavian, William Mann wrote in *The Times*: "The star was unquestionably Janet Baker's Octavian. She has some *travesti* parts in her repertory; this one is the most demanding, and the most rewarding too. She can exert her femininity as Mariandl; her drunken wailing in the pub scene is deliciously sung without a trace of burlesque, indeed all of a piece with the first-act dialogue after the Marschallin's soliloquy about the clock-stopping, with the Presentation of the Rose. It was Miss Baker who held the famous trio, and the marvellous music before and after it, together, inspiring her colleagues and hitting her audience where it hurts most, delightfully. Miss Baker sang the English text most intelligibly of all and made it sound most realistic."

And Desmond Shawe-Taylor commented: "Janet Baker's Octavian was the most successful and the most clearly enunciated performance of the evening."

In-between these Scottish Opera performances came Janet's success in another comic role—Diana at Glyndebourne in Cavalli's *La Calisto*, produced by Peter Hall and conducted by Raymond Leppard, in the summer of 1970. In this role she has to impersonate not only the Goddess herself but also Jupiter masquerading as Diana in order to seduce the nymph Callisto. Leppard illustrated Janet's North Country directness and her clarity of her mind by what happened before this production. "We originally intended that the bass portraying Jupiter should also play himself as Diana. He could sing it perfectly well but it turned out to be very 'camp'. After a week of rehearsals Peter and I decided to ask if Janet would consider doing the disguised Jupiter as well as her part. Remember, there were only three weeks to go until the first night. She asked for ten minutes to think about it and then agreed to do it. That is the sort of decision she is able to make and you have the confidence that if she says she will do it, she can.

"She also has this ability to colour her voice in a particular way. I remember more recently when she has worked with me on *Poppaea* at the Coliseum, in the scene where she gets a promise from Nero that he might dispense with Ottavia she says; 'Go now' or whatever is the English equivalent. At first she sang this passage very romantically but I thought that this was a place

Top: As Marguerite in 'The Damnation of Faust' at the Coliseum, 1971 with Alberto Remedios as Faust and Raimund Herincx as Mephistopheles. [Reg Wilson

Above: As Monteverdi's Poppaea at the Coliseum, 1971. [Dominic

35

where you can feel the coldness of the character so I asked her to make her tone sound 'flinty'. At that moment, the audience should sense the power of this woman—she is already for a second the boss and a nasty piece of work—and Janet did it wonderfully.

"Janet is a great worker on her own, so that when she comes to rehearsals she already has a very good idea of her role: she is on terms with it from the very beginning. She is also a natural actress. I remember Peter Hall saying when we rehearsed *Calisto* that she can stand on the stage and *is* of the stage. Mood and feeling seem to come absolutely naturally. And she achieves her effects without too much movement.

"She has a very firm will. She works very hard but she knows her own limits and will not exceed them. If she has a performance or recital at night, she quite definitely will not rehearse during the day—and quite right too. I have never toured with her, but I know that she found her first American trip—when she was sent to all the backwaters—terribly tiring. For a fortnight after she was in a bad mood. She is very excitable and forthright about that kind of thing. I think she told Hurok's that if they wanted her back, they would have to change their ways where she was concerned." Janet confirms that she is very particular about where she will sing in America. On the other hand, if some very small place has shown her special kindness, she will go out of her way to return there.

Leppard also said that Janet is very nervous before a performance: "She gets into a real state, particularly before a recital. On the stage she seems better able to contain her nerves."

Her appearance as Penelope in Monteverdi's *Il Ritorno d'Ulisse in Patria* at 1972 Glyndebourne was another universally acclaimed success. Andrew Porter wrote that "Miss Baker, on stage, is made of other stuff than ordinary mortals. There is no one like her. Throughout the evening she holds us rapt . . . Miss Baker's Penelope is ineffably beautiful and eloquent both to hear and watch. She is the steady flame at the heart of a noble performance".

Janet is very anxious to divide her time carefully in the future between her various activities. "Opera has been encroaching more and more over the past few years, and I keep getting offers from all over the place so that I could now have a solely operatic career. I also want to be at home much more. I want to be a person who has a life in which music plays a very important part but not an all-absorbing one. Up to now, I have naturally felt my career had to come first. I do not mean to say music will no longer be important to me—of course, it will, until the day I die—but it is a jealous taskmaster and I begin to resent that. I want to be a person who also happens to be a musician—which simply means I want to do less performances a year. Physically and mentally, it is a great strain appearing so often as one grows older. I just must have more time for living—and you cannot have that if you are travelling and studying. There is no time to dig my garden—and I want to be able to do that. And see my friends and be within my own four walls. Perhaps that sounds really ungrateful—and I do appreciate everything that has happened to me.

"People's lives are divided into certain patterns—like the times of the year. Right from being a baby, a person is at a certain age, a certain stage. During each period of time, certain things happen that should allow them to develop, and I can see at this moment in time, I am moving from one stage into another. I do not know whether I should be feeling like that. All I can say to you is that I am more and more determined that my life should not be dominated by flying around the world in aircraft, wearing myself out, and giving myself all of the time. It is just too tiring. I know, as I have always known, that I must go on giving back my gift to people, but I do not think it is any more important singing in Carnegie Hall than it used to be to Welsh audiences in the early days. There comes a time when this thing, people call success, which brings a degree of fame whatever that may mean, and of financial independence—and I am certainly fulfilled and a happy human being—is not all. There must be nothing that stops me living the pattern of life as a total person. And there is no doubt that musicians *do* compartmentalise themselves. In a way, we are awfully fortunate because being a performer teaches one to think about the world and one's relationships with other people in a very deep way, so that if I am aware that my life is moving from one stage to another, it is because I have been in music that I am aware of it. And it is not really music that I want to cut out of life—it is the success bit. The outside pressures on you are killers: your values are in terrible danger. You actually begin to think: 'Who is this per-

As Penelope with Benjamin Luxon as Ulysses in Monteverdi's 'Il Ritorno d'Ulisse in Patria' at Glyndebourne, 1972. [Guy Gravett

son called Janet Baker? Well, she is a well-known singer, but where does that leave the real me.' I'm not expressing this very well—but I do feel a danger that my work will get out of proportion. I must not let it mean more than it really does.

"I know that if you do not achieve anything in life, you never arrive at this stage: I am very lucky to be able to say this right now. Maybe because of this I am being pushed into a different view of life. It is just a question of re-stating your values under the pressure of being a world-wide commuter and being constantly in the public's eye. You just have to keep on telling yourself that you are no more than an ordinary person doing your job. You must not be taken over by things outside your own control. People say if you have a lovely career and make the grade, that is it—no problems. It *is* marvellous—and I am not underestimating its enormous advantages—but it produces its own problems, and they are terribly dangerous ones, so you are in a more vulnerable position because of it."

CHARACTER AND PHILOSOPHY

"I have always been a strong character, ever since my childhood. My mother says I was almost wilful and that she had to be very firm with me, or else I would have tried to rule her. My brother was someone who could be reasoned with; I was someone who had to learn the hard way. I have to experience something and learn from that experience. I know I feel very strongly that people must think things out for themselves. They must do them from a sincere, real point of view and not be shoved into them because they happen to be good at something at school. They must be taught how to discover themselves. If someone has not an outstanding aptitude at some-

At Expo '70 in Japan with John Pritchard.

thing, how do you guide them? They must be shown the right way of assessing themselves. Our attitude to what people should try to achieve is wrong, the attitude towards money and success, keeping up with the Joneses, and I would like to know how we could get rid of it. Maybe that is what young people today are trying to find out. But they must try not to fall into the other extreme of not caring what they do with their lives; they must try to do something constructive about it."

Janet reads a great deal. "Books are in a sense my life—mostly psychology and philosophy. I derive my ideas from them; they continually open new windows, new facets of the world. At least some people have this ability to make you see things in a new light. And I think these ideas can be brought to my music, and can improve and change it as can meeting people and the different circumstances one constantly finds oneself in. A marvellous thing about life is this continual process of assimilation in order to give something out again. Performers, if they can find this secret of 'giving out', are also finding one of the answers to happiness. I believe, though, that everyone does have this chance if they have examined themselves closely enough to discover it, and not be coerced into doing anything for the wrong reason. It must be a deeply-felt, interior matter. How do you start that process? I do not quite know. As far as I am concerned, perhaps something happened as a child that I do not remember which gave me the key to it. I am sure that even if I were not singing, I would be equally fulfilled and happy doing something else—maybe writing."

As an interpreter, she tries to stand aside and watch herself. "You split yourself up into two people—one bit is outside watching the process, the other bit, inside the process, that is performing, is so totally engrossed that there is room for nothing else. This may sound like a contradiction, but I think any performer will know what I mean. You see, you must not actually get bogged down in emotion or you cannot give anything out; one side of the personality controls that, while the other side works with the trained equipment plus something that is God-given, the magic moment when, say, a Schubert phrase, through you, is made alive. An audience, of course, affects you; indeed, I am perhaps too much affected by them. If I am not at ease, or I think they are expecting too much of me, as they do when you get to a certain stage, that can affect you. I try not to care, but it is probably because I *do* care about them, that I do reach them for a lot of the time. And, of course, every performance is different depending on the circumstances out there and what may have happened to me during the day.

"Although my own records, once done, no longer interest me because they are frozen, static performances, I do listen to other people's. I like orchestral and chamber works for relaxation, because I am not then listening in a critical way. I do not listen to singing because I cannot get sheer pleasure from the music. If I am listening at home, I do want to enjoy myself."

Janet has very definite ideas about modern music. "I have not the necessary equipment for singing new works as I would want to do them. You must have perfect pitch to make sure you are going to land on a certain

[EMI

note. If I could master that problem, I am sure I could make musical sense to myself out of avant-garde pieces, but beyond a certain stage, I am so mixed-up about pitch worries that I am not free to perform the works properly. It's like those singers who never get beyond the stage of worrying about technique. If I am ever concerned about whether I am going to reach a note or not, there is no chance of interpretation. So feeling fettered by the technical difficulties because of my own inadequacy in this respect, I cannot undertake this music, and it would be wrong for me to do it."

Janet does not practise in the abstract, but whenever she is going to give a performance or to record, she will first warm up her voice. "Otherwise, I try to rest it as much as possible."

In performing on the stage, she follows a very definite practice. "I try to listen to the actual words others are singing to me and react as though I were hearing them for the first time. If possible I like to re-create the situation anew each time. I attempt to put out of mind everything that has happened before and make that particular sentence or action something fresh. If the other artist is doing the same thing, it can be a wonderful experience. For the audience to share this experience, it is obviously preferable for them to understand every word. To that extent, I like to sing opera in English. The difference was most marked between performances of *Calisto* at Glyndebourne, where the laughs were few because no one understood the comedy, and the Prom performance afterwards when the audience had a detailed synopsis in front of them, and could follow and enjoy the comedy. Immediately the whole performance took off because we were playing to an audience that was getting every phrase. I think you must choose the vern-

acular until people are educated enough in the work to follow it in the original. For instance, I think Scottish audiences could now take *Così* in Italian. Nobody denies that every work loses something in translation, but what is the point of performing *Rosenkavalier*, with all its verbal subtleties, to an audience that is not following the German text? It is a battle in which we all take different sides, I know. Many people think that where music is involved, words do not matter, but a performer who feels people's attention wandering has an awful problem. An audience whose mind is wandering is a tangible thing."

Janet is interested in all homely things—except cooking. "I have no interest in it, but one day, when I retire, I hope to have a go at it. As far as dresses and hair styles are concerned, I like a frequent change. In this visual age, I think it is important to look more or less right, to try and look your best. People are 'tele-conscious' today and they will not accept the awful way some recitalists used to get themselves up. I also like costumes that make me look right on the platform. I have no help in that respect. I always get myself ready and choose my own hair and dress style—right or wrong. For stage make-up I try to use as little as possible. I have to accentuate my bone-structure, which is not good, to draw it on for the sake of stage lighting. My face is rather flat. Bearing that in mind, I do the same sort of thing in a modified form for the concert platform, to create light and dark, contours if you like. I have a struggle not to put on weight, and as soon as I take some off, I seem to put it on again. Although I may not like cooking food, I adore eating it. The trouble is that when we are away, we cannot control what we eat. I am very conscious of weight as a matter of fitness."

Of Janet's future, Lord Harewood speaks with the greatest enthusiasm and expectancy. He looks forward before long to hearing her not only in the Rossini parts already mentioned but also as Carmen, Fricka, Elizabeth in *Gloriana* and even Amneris. "As long ago as 1966 or 1967, when Klemperer was considering his cast for a complete *Walküre*—unfortunately only the first act was completed—he had Janet in mind for Fricka. I feel certain that she is now ready to tackle the Wagner parts, Brangäne as well as Fricka.

"As a recitalist I am sure she is expanding her repertory all the time. She is a fine linguist. With practice most people can sing Italian and German, but I am amazed how excellent her French is—when I heard her first record of French songs, I thought that she must have been brought up in France, That is really a remarkable achievement. She would be marvellous as Padmâvati in Roussel's opera, a beautiful piece that needs a singer just like Janet and a really good production to make it succeed. Doing a work like that, which is not a certain success, with Janet would be less of a risk because she could take half the responsibility. If she takes on a role, she knows that she will be able to sing it successfully, because she can analyse every step in her career and know exactly what it will do to her voice. She will also take tremendous pains over whatever she does. That is why it is such a pity that we 'pussyfoot' in this country over our casting and do not take the risks they do abroad. Janet is an enlarging artist and we must make the most of her."

🌿 *Recording and* 🌿 *Repertory*

Janet thinks that her early records have a particular quality of freshness that is perhaps no longer there. She considers her more recent ones to be valid in a different way. "There's something about a young singer's approach to music that is sweet. The instrument sounds fresh. You are a young person doing music and there is always something touching about that. I remember making the *Frauenliebe* cycle for Saga in a funny little church just round the corner. It was an occasion for me, and I tried to forget all about the technical side and just sing my best. I had the same approach to the job as I do now: every 'take' must be considered a final 'take'. That may be the reason that, when I am making solo discs, I can record so quickly. I do not like the business of going over and over small details—you must keep some sort of performance in view.

"I found recording very tiring—and I still do. I am certain that one session in a day is quite enough. I think it is a hard physical and mental strain. But I like recording because I have had a lot of experience with a microphone in front of me at the BBC, and I do not mind not having an audience. It's a different kind of concentration. I find that the longer a session goes on the less critical I become—I can no longer hear so much because I become brainwashed by the sound, and the longer the 'takes' go, the more one loses that essential freshness of approach.

[*EMI*

"There is no question that canned music of any kind has its dangers. However excellent a disc may be, there is bound to be one dimension missing, because of the absence of the person. I never heard or saw Kathleen Ferrier in the flesh, and everyone says how much one misses from not seeing that exceptional woman on the platform."

Certain works have become particularly associated with Janet, such as *Frauenliebe und Leben*, which was one of her earliest recordings. "It's a work that has been with me all my singing life. I have sung it so often that when I am doing it with Martin Isepp, we do not even bother to rehearse it. The banal quality of the poems does not worry me because I do not think about them in that sort of way. I just take off and let Schumann do the rest. I keep the songs as simple and serious as I can without thinking about the drawbacks of the sentiments being expressed. Without a doubt it always comes off, if

43

I am in the right frame of mind, because it is a spontaneous sort of piece. "I have found that records have lifted my career on to a different plane, like my first American tour some years ago. I now find that wherever I go I have an audience even though I may never have been there before, and that is something tremendous."

"From *Gerontius* onwards, I fell in love with her as everyone does" was how Kinloch Anderson, producer of many of Janet's EMI records, described the beginning of their working relationship. "She has this extraordinary quality not only of singing beautifully and having a marvellous technique—she just makes you adore her, to a degree that I have never come across in any other artist. I know Janet does not like being compared with Kathleen Ferrier but I am sure Ferrier had that same quality. I think she has, like Ferrier, an immediacy of approach to the listener, even in a large hall. She has the ability of making each individual member of the audience feel that she is singing just for them.

"As far as recording is concerned, I never cease to be amazed at the high standard she will maintain however often something is repeated because she has not been satisfied with it previously. I think that the voice sits naturally, that she has an almost inborn technical command, and an extraordinary self-discipline. Recording with her is always such fun that I often feel that it is a pity I cannot be working with her every day, especially when she and Gerald Moore are together, because they have a kind of game of insulting each other in a playful way that is delightful.

"In the studio she has tremendous stamina. So many singers are continuously worried that they are going to do damage to their voices. She will go on until she has got as near to her own exigent standards. When making recital records, she prefers to work longer sessions. Rather than four of three hours, she chooses three sessions of four hours—simply because once she has

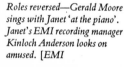

Roles reversed—Gerald Moore sings with Janet 'at the piano'. Janet's EMI recording manager Kinloch Anderson looks on amused. [EMI

begun, she likes to go on. I think she knows that she has her voice under such control that she is not going to ruin it. On the whole she can go on longer producing higher standards of vocalisation than any other singer I have come across. As far as 'takes' are concerned, one usually repeats to satisfy her rather than others. Sometimes it is true I want her to do something again because a word has gone wrong or I want her to phrase something in a single breath—she once told me 'You never want me to breathe, do you?— but very often if we do a song twice that suffices.

"She is one of the most objective artists I know. She has a very good assessment of what she can, and what she cannot, do. She knows how good she is, of course, but she also knows her own limitations. That is why she has practically never attempted anything that is too heavy for her. She is very well aware that she has not an enormous voice, not one that she can pit against a very large orchestra, so she wisely leaves that alone. Then, she is such a well-adjusted person, it is almost too good to be true; but how delightful to find that it *is* in fact true. Whether she is grilling bacon over her own stove or being a great actress, I can hardly criticise her. Of all the many things we have done together, the only ones I would slightly fault are some of the Strauss songs in one of the Lieder recitals. I suppose one could imagine them being done more sensuously—but this possible lack is weighed down on the other side by so many fine qualities. With her singing, you do not just give way to the sheer sensuous beauty of the voice because there are so many other points to admire. Her voice is slightly astringent and that is something I like enormously.

"Her French singing is extraordinary in someone who does not speak the language fluently. When we were recording *The Damnation of Faust* in Paris, she was a little worried about singing with such marvellous French-speaking artists, so she wanted someone to check her French. My Paris colleague, quite a strict man, agreed to listen with this in mind. After the first take or two, he had not said anything, so I asked him to make some comment. He replied that there was not anything to correct—it was mar-vellous French singing. She must have a very acute ear for languages and she, of course, takes tremendous trouble to get it right."

Kinloch Anderson got to know Janet before she or he had been on the EMI books. He did a South Place concert with her in the late 1950s of the Brahms *Liebeslieder Walzer* in which he and Bernice Lehmann were the pianists and Janet was the alto soloist. "Ilse Wolf undertook to get the quartet together and sang soprano herself, the tenor was Edgar Fleet and the baritone John Shirley-Quirk. I had never heard Janet before and I was greatly impressed. From that moment on I watched her art develop."

OPERA

At present Janet Baker's operatic recordings are relatively few; one must hope that this situation is rectified over the next few years. Such that there be are all worth having, each assumption revealing afresh her extensive gift for characterisation. Two of them remind us of her collaboration, already touched upon, with the English Opera Group. The more important of these is her interpretation of the title role in Britten's *The Rape of Lucretia*. When she sang the part with the E.O.G. in Liverpool in 1966, Stanley Sadie commented in *The Times*: "Their success tonight was due to the intense impersonation of Lucretia by Miss Janet Baker. She acted her first scene like a woman transfigured by love pre-echoing Lucretia's words in the morning-after scene. The complex of her emotions in the rape was caught with fearsome clarity and her final outburst was movingly impassioned. Miss Baker's enunciation of both music and words was beautifully clear."

The recording, made at the Maltings, Snape, is a true facsimile of her stage performance. You feel the sense of doomed expectancy, even of slight boredom, at "How quiet it is tonight". The phrases beginning "Oh my beloved Collatinus" show the richness of her lower register. Then in the rape scene, the tone takes on a tremulous, anguished note, particularly at "though I am in your arms". But the interpretation reaches its greatest intensity, rightly, in the last scene, where the voice seems to change colour and become darker, even hollow, until it revives in the bitter consolation of "To love as we loved", her sad words to her understanding husband. To quote Stanley Sadie again, this time in his review of the records: Janet's singing has a "marvellous, luminous integrity: still, concentrated, intense, but with a hint of passion". Without question, this is one of the most moving operatic portrayals of our time.

Kate in *Owen Wingrave* is a very different kind of part and Janet shows her versatility by creating, for once, a thoroughly unsympathetic character. Kate is a strong-willed, firm, rather complacent girl, certain that she is right in wanting Owen to forsake his silly pacifist ideas and instead follow his forefathers to the wars. With her superb diction, Janet ferociously spits out such phrases as "I'd say that you weren't good enough" and "We need no teaching from a boy". There is even hatred in "What you do and what you think has ceased to interest us". Yet you feel, and naturally Britten has much to do with this, that behind the callousness and unkindness, to which the tutor's wife, Mrs Coyle, refers, there is a certain inner vulnerability to Kate. Janet shows this side of the character in her solo and in the single line "Yes, I've lost something". Then at the end her grief and remorse are powerfully expressed by those piercing, anguished cries heard by the Coyle's from their bedroom, when Kate finds Owen dead in the haunted room. Indeed, she does much to justify the somewhat incredible ending.

Janet's expected recording of the title role in *Gloriana* should complete a notable hat-trick of Britten discs conducted by the composer for Decca.

Her performance on the Argo set of Cavalli's *La Calisto* commemorated her portrayal at Glyndebourne of Diana, and Jove-as-Diana, in the 1970 and 1971 seasons there. She is not afraid in this 17th-century music to use the full range of expressiveness at her command, bringing glorious opulence to the aria "Ardo, sospiro e piango" and warm, sensual tones to her seduction of Calisto—"con la dolcezza de' naci tuoi". In the aria "Amara servitù", imported by Raymond Leppard from another Cavalli work, her emotional range is quite searing, then she fines away her tone to a half-voice at "Soave libertà".

After playing Jove-as-Diana, Janet cleverly contrasts the real Diana's outrage when approached by Calisto with loving intentions of a distinctly dubious kind, and conveys this by the disgust in her tone at "Taci, lasciva, taci". Yet another mood, one of intimate adoration, is conveyed in the amorous scenes of Diana (as herself) with Endymion, particularly in the whispered phrases "Mio sole, addio", where Janet fines her tone away to nothing, an effect she also achieved in the closing duet of *Poppaea* at the Coliseum. Finally, there is a touch of the heroic in her saving of Endymion from the wrath of Pan near the end of the opera. There was much humour in her stage portrayal and, although much is missed on records, those who have also seen the production will be able to recall it in their mind's eye.

Janet's earliest operatic record was *Dido and Aeneas* under Anthony Lewis's direction. We have already seen how the recording came about. It was highly successful and remains, in most people's books, the most satisfying of the many versions available. At the time when the record first appeared, Edward Greenfield wrote prophetically in *The Guardian*: "Let me begin with the Dido, Janet Baker, who on this showing at least can set her sights on almost any peak. She is usually described as a contralto, and her lower register is certainly rich and firm enough, if without any trace of plumminess, but cannot someone lead her out on top to full soprano stature, just as Richard Bonynge led the unsuspecting Sutherland half a stave higher into a range she never knew she had? The part of Dido at least requires nothing higher than a G and Miss Baker's stylishness, range of tone colour, depth of emotion implied with no untidy gusts all reveal a natural command that promises great things. In the final, tragic scene, the contrast between the angry, majestic words 'Away, away' to the weak Aeneas and the dark grief of 'But death I cannot shun' is wonderfully achieved—dramatic soprano tone-colour contrasting with deliberately darkened contralto. Just as impressive and even more subtle is the contrast when the opening phrase 'When I am laid in earth' is repeated a few bars on, a model of graduated *mezza voce*. Then with the words 'Remember me' in a monotone Miss Baker subdues her natural vibrato to produce a white tone of hushed, aching intensity. I shall be surprised to hear a more deeply satisfying interpretation of this greatest of arias. 'Ah, Belinda' is just as beautiful with deliciously delicate grace-notes on the phrase 'Peace and I'."

I would only add to that comprehensive review that she fully conveys the onomatopoeia at the word "languish" in that first aria and the determination of "Your counsel all is urged in vain," and that she moves perfectly from the B flat to E flat on the word "create" in the noble lament at the end. Everywhere on this record, phrasing and words are re-thought with that vividness and care for meaning that distinguish Janet's work from that of lesser singers. Sir Anthony Lewis's contribution to her achievement should, incidentally, not be overlooked.

As Dido at Drottningholm.

They collaborated again in Rameau's *Hippolyte et Aricie*, this time recorded, in 1965, immediately after stage performances at the Barber Institute in Birmingham. As the tragic heroine Phèdre, she shows her usual understanding of changing dramatic situations—jealousy of Aricie for loving Phèdre's step-son Hippolyte with whom she herself is infatuated, delight when she thinks her husband Theseus is dead (so that she will now be free to form a liaison with Hippolyte). Her longing for him is beautifully caught in the aria "Cruelle mère des amours", where text is precisely matched to tone. Her remorse after Hippolyte's death again finds an expressive response from Janet. Phèdre was written for a soprano but, as Andrew Porter commented in *The Financial Times*: "The role of Phèdre lies high for Janet Baker yet she contrives almost to make a virtue of strain and her glowing, passionate performance is powerfully affecting."

Another operatic disc from Janet, made about the same time, was Holst's, *Savitri*, with Imogen Holst as conductor, and it is one I particularly treasure. In the title role, the Woodcutter's Wife who by will and love repels the figure of Death, come to claim her husband, Janet once more demonstrates her ability to run through a wide range of tone colour, adopting a bleak, sad sound for "The world has now become a grave", resigned and self-possessed for "Welcome, Lord", and affirming for "Life is eternal Greater than thou". Again there is that wonderful use of words, nowhere more touching than in the tender solo "Without thee I am as the dead". All roles no doubt bring out a part of a good singer's personality; here the strength of character and firmness of will that represent Savitri seem also to represent the artist. What a wonderful English double-bill this and *Dido* would make with Janet in the main parts, if someone had the courage to stage it.

Janet Baker's sole recordings in the field of opera for EMI have been of Berlioz, if we include for convenience purposes *Le Damnation de Faust* as an opera here. As the other Dido, of the second part of *Les Troyens*, we have only the last two scenes recorded shortly after the Scottish Opera performances in 1969 with Alexander Gibson, who was in the pit at Glasgow on that memorable night. Dido, self-pitying but still surely, deeply in love at first, fills with bitter anger, then hatred when she realises that Aeneas is really going to leave her. All this is fully encompassed in Janet Baker's interpretation and inflected in fine French. The insensate fury of the cries "Ah, Ah" lead on to the extraordinary variations of tone colour as the heroine takes her decision to die. After the burning intensity of "A la mort tout entière" comes the sad farewell "Adieu, fière cité" and the tender recollection of the love duet. In the final, sacrificial scene there is ecstasy in the famous, prophetic cries of "Hannibal".

Janet recorded Marguerite in *Damnation* before she had sung the part on the stage, at the Coliseum with Sadler's Wells Opera in 1971. Lest my own opinions may be thought uniquely euphoric, I quote what Harold Rosenthal, editor of *Opera* had to say about the stage assumption: "Although Marguerite's contribution to the Berlioz version of the *Faust* legend is comparatively short, Miss Baker's made it the central part of the drama. Her

Talking with Nicolai Gedda during sessions for Berlioz's 'La Damnation de Faust' in Paris. [EMI

committed and sensual singing and acting, especially of 'D'amour l'ardente flamme', which opened the second part of the evening, and her contribution to the trio that closed the second half take a very high place on my select list of great operatic experiences."

The records support that claim. Although Lionel Salter in *The Gramophone* was not exactly complimentary about the set as a whole, he was unstinted in his praise for Janet "who from her very first notes exactly hits the right character and mood for Marguerite . . . She sounds young and innocent her voice is fresh, perfectly focussed and subtly coloured, and her words are used with clarity and imagination: I do not have to labour the point of Miss Baker's great artistry". These points are most arrestingly exemplified in the short, broken phrases at the end of The King of Thule *chanson gothique*. Berlioz wrote this part for a mezzo and not for the soprano more usually heard in it. The fullness of tone, warm timbre that Janet provides seem to suit it exactly.

BACH AND HANDEL

There are those who believe that Janet's singing of Bach and Handel are the summit of her achievement, and certainly if I was forced to take only one aspect of her art on to a desert island it would have to be her records, as yet all too few, of Bach cantatas. Most of her admirers will know her Bach singing through the yearly performances of the *St Matthew Passion*, either in German with Paul Steinitz and his London Bach Society or in English with   [EMI

David Willcocks and the Bach Choir, and it is almost beyond compre-
hension that she has yet to record a version of this work. I urge those who
attend these annual events, but have so far fought shy of investigating the
cantatas, to buy the HMV and Oiseau-Lyre discs containing three of the solo
ones.

One of her abiding virtues as a Bach singer is that she does not seem to
have to worry at all about technique. Where with other artists one is often
worried whether they will be able to get their voices round the runs or
manage to stay in tune during some of those fiendishly difficult leaps, with
Janet you can sit back in the realisation that all will be well. She herself
obviously has absolute confidence in what she is doing otherwise she would
not be able to give such wholehearted attention to matters of nuance,
phrasing and words.

ASD2302, with Menuhin and the Bath Festival Orchestra, has on one
side the Cantata No. 169 where a gentle, light arioso, alternating with
recitative, leads into an aria with organ obbligato (the immaculate Simon
Preston), "Gott soll allein mein Herze haben", where Janet as always is
incomparable in expressing a sense of inner elation, particularly here at the
words "das höchste Gut" ("my greatest joy"). There is inwardness too in the
succeeding recitative where the question "What is the love of God?" is
consolingly answered by the words "Rest for the mind, joy for the heart".
In the second aria, one of Bach's other-worldly sicilianos, the runs are very
even and the tone marvellously warm and sympathetic. In the final recitative
there is a splendid certainty in the affirmation, "Thou shalt love God and thy
neighbour".

On the reverse, Janet sings *Ich habe genug*, Cantata No. 82, usually sung
by a bass. Bach allowed the alto alternative and Janet shows that the work is
just as apt for her kind of voice. Alec Robertson summed up her performance
in *The Gramophone* by saying: "What a joy to have a singer who understands
all about appoggiaturas, and has such a true feeling for words and moulding
of phrases". He then went on to make some detailed points with which I
entirely concur. "Miss Baker's singing of the recitative and arioso before
the exquisite slumber song is profoundly moving, and nowhere more so
than the change of tone she makes after 'Let us go with this man' to the
hushed plea 'O Lord, from my body's chains release me'. Most lovely, too,
is her singing of the descending phrase at the close of the rondo theme in
'Schlummert ein', and at the words 'Süsser Friede, stille Ruh' before the final
repeat."

In the first aria the word "begierigen" ("eager") is quite individually
inflected and the divisions in the exceedingly difficult last aria are turned into
part of the expression, a mark of the truly discerning Bach singer. Michael
Dobson is the fine oboe obbligato player in the first and last arias.

Oiseau-Lyre SOL295, is, if possible, even more indispensable as an example
of Janet's art as a Bach singer and I do not think any other disc has caught
the beauty of her voice so ideally. This record, made in February 1966, was
her first of Bach and it had the inestimable support of Neville Marriner and

the Academy of St Martin's. On the first side she is joined by two other fine Bach artists, Robert Tear and John Shirley-Quirk, in the original, even for Bach, Cantata No. 159, *Sehet, wir gehn hinauf gen Jerusalem!*, which begins, as Desmond Shawe-Taylor put it "with the alto solo questioning, pleading, attempting to delay the quiet onward movement of the solo bass's aria, and follows this 'two-level' piece with another, in which the alto's aria proceeds against the startling interventions of the chorus sopranos with the well-known Passion chorale". In the latter, Janet's radiant singing again seems like an expression of faith.

On the other side she tackles the solo cantata, No. 170 *Vergnügte Ruh*, where the opening slumber song matches in beauty that in *Ich habe genug*. In the first recitative there is again varying of tone and incisive enunciation of the text; even more so at the words "Ich zittre recht und fühle tausend Schmerzen" ("I am frightened and feel a thousand hurts") in the extraordinarily vivid account of the searching second aria with its chromatic organ obbligato acutely played by Philip Ledger. The final aria, one of rejoicing, finds a tripping, brilliant response from the singer.

Janet plays a smaller part in the two cantata disc made with Wolfgang Gönnenwein, whom I find a rather dull Bach conductor. In No. 148, her outstanding contribution comes in the technical ease with which she dispatches her arias with the words on the tone and the runs neatly executed. No. 149 has a delightful duet with the tenor and an unusual bassoon obbligato. Listen to Janet's attack on the repeated phrases "Seid wachsam", a model for all Bach singers. A pity the recording does not do justice to her voice.

In the recording, under Barenboim of the *Magnificat* her contribution may be small but it is very significant. In the "Esurientes", what William Mann calls the "delicious, lolling pastoral" Janet sings with just the right limpid tone and unforced simplicity, emphasising delightfully the word "inanes" ("empty"), where the rich are sent empty away. The two-flute accompaniment is subtly matched to the voice. Janet also contributes to the succeeding trio, a smoothly flowing movement where her voice blends well with those of Lucia Popp and Anne Pashley.

Janet makes an invaluable contribution to several major recordings of choral works. In the B minor Mass under Klemperer, her radiant "Laudamus te", neatly embellished, is followed by a flowing account of the lovely "Qui sedes" and a moving one of "Agnus dei", surely sustained at the conductor's very deliberate tempo. Pavlova's alleged statement that one learns technique only so one can forget about it comes to mind when listening to this effortless, seamless singing. Britain has a long-standing tradition of fine Bach style, but I doubt if this solo has ever been sung with such grave beauty.

In Mendelssohn's *Elijah* the peacefulness of "O Rest in the Lord" is finely projected, the singer's lightweight reading of this well-worn aria freeing it from unhappy associations with the hooty brigade. "Woe unto me" has the right urgency to it, with wonderful consolation coming in the tender middle section. Janet changes the character of her tone to portray the few but significant phrases of the evil Queen, urging on her people to kill the prophet.

Janet's subordination of her very positive personality in the service of ensemble work is manifest in the recordings of Beethoven's Mass in C, under Giulini, and the Mozart *Requiem* (there is far too little of Janet in Mozart on disc, incidentally) and the blend with Sheila Armstrong, Nicolai Gedda and Fischer-Dieskau in the "Recordare" of the *Requiem* is near-ideal. When she does step into the limelight as for the few phrases beginning "Judex ergo" in the "Tuba mirum", her singing has all its usual urgency: "Nil inultum remanebit" ("nothing shall remain unavenged") is a forceful statement of fact as here delivered.

Handel, as already noted, is just as much Baker territory as Bach, and it is a pity that as yet none of her interpretations of mezzo and castrato roles in his operas is available on record. As consolation, we have the exciting disc of two of the solo cantatas. Janet sang these at a Queen Elizabeth Hall concert at the end of 1967, and I clearly recall the all-embracing effect of her interpretations on her audience. For once the gramophone enables one to re-live a memorable experience. Although, of course, this record was made later, in the studio it recaptures the essence of those performances: the complete emotional commitment of the singer expressed through a well-nigh faultless technique.

Both cantatas were written for soprano but there is little or no feeling of strain in encompassing the sometimes quite high tessitura, and the rich, tensely focused tone often adds a dimension to these works that a lighter voice could not manage. Each has three arias, alternating with passages of

Recording the Mozart 'Requiem' with producer Suvi Raj Grubb. [EMI

recitative. It goes almost without saying that, as was usually the case in pieces of this nature in the baroque era, the cantatas are concerned with ladies having problems of an amorous nature, and the various arias express in turn anger, resignation, delight for each of which Handel finds unerringly the appropriate music. The tragic opening aria of *Ah! crudel, nel pianto mio* and the eloquent middle aria of *Armida abbandonata* are perhaps the most daringly written and they are wonderfully sung. Perhaps the cantatas should not be played one after the other because then the tremendous intensity of the performances can seem overbearing. Divided, say, by a baroque concerto, they are ideal.

For the present Janet has renounced *Messiah*, which seems a pity when you hear her accounts of the contralto arias on the Mackerras set. You can immediately hear what we are missing by listening to her first recitative where the old, familiar words and music sound for once new-minted. The, single "Emmanuel" is a bold declaration in itself. In "O thou that tellest" the decorations seem naturally part of the line, which is how it should be, and the injunctions "Arise, shine" are glowingly projected. In "He shall feed his flock", she adopts a limpid, gentle delivery that is most appealing. "He was despised" is suitably grave and sad. In the middle section the consonants are rightly accentuated on such words as "smiters" and "spitting". In the reprise the embellishments may go too far for some tastes, but they are certainly executed with ease and authority. In this authentic *Messiah*, the editors, Mackerras and Basil Lam, have gone back to the version of "How beautiful are the feet" for contralto, counter-tenor and chorus that was used at the first performance (although the autograph score has the more familiar

Checking a point with Charles Mackerras during the 'Messiah' sessions. [EMI

soprano aria). Janet's voice combines nicely here with Paul Esswood's. In that remarkably invigorating early work, *Dixit Dominus*, the solo work is secondary to the choral but Janet makes the most of the elaborate, rather unrewarding "Virga virtutis tuae".

A substantial pendant to this collection of Janet's records of baroque music is the one with music by the two Scarlattis and Monteverdi. This has been variously and adversely criticised because of the very elaborate Leppard accompaniments and because it was felt Janet brought to this music a depth of feeling probably beyond what the composers intended. I would not dispute the first point: the elaborate string and keyboard support, at least as reverberantly recorded here, does sometimes overload and detract from the vocal line. As far as the second point is concerned, I find the emotional variety in Queen Ottavia's two solos from Monteverdi's *L'incoronazione di Poppea* takes them right away from the history books and into the realm of living art. Besides, Janet is better suited to this part than to that of Poppaea, which she played at the Coliseum, or at least it seems more naturally hers. She evokes even more sympathy than is usual for the one sympathetic, upright character in the opera. Accusing, remorseful, and sorrowful by turns, her performances stir the heart. The emotions are certainly writ large but that is surely what the composer *did* want here. The passions are grand, too, in Ariadne's Lament, with clear division between the full voice used for the recitative and the half voice for the passages of arioso. You feel that a real actor-singer is at work throughout the Monteverdi parts of this disc.

She cannot do much for the rather dull *Salve Regina* of Domenico Scarlatti, but his father's beautiful *Christmas Cantata* is sung with lovely, fresh tone and radiant expression, also consummate technical control. In the final aria, a gentle pastoral, her simple, intimate singing is beyond reproach. To this disc must be added her sure account of the "Domine deus" in the Argo recording at King's College of Vivaldi's *Gloria*.

GERMAN AND FRENCH SONG

The concomitant of Janet's wish not to specialise is that she is about as versatile a singer as there is to be found today, and her records reflect this. For instance, no British singer that I can recall has ranged so far over the Lieder field. Her most ambitious project to date is the two-disc Schubert evening, surely planned by HMV as a kind of substantial pendant to Fischer-Dieskau's vast boxes of Schubert songs on Deutsche Grammophon, for most of the songs are specifically ones written for a woman. Schubert's delightful *Suleika* settings and the atmospheric group from Sir Walter Scott's *Lady of the Lake* are perhaps the peaks of this album and Baker's performances make me wonder why they are so seldom encountered in recital programmes. In the Scott set, the consistently held mood of intimacy in "Raste, Krieger" Gerald Moore's imitation of a bugle in "Jäger, ruhe von der Jagd" and Janet's subtle varying of her tone for each verse of "Ave Maria" display the art of

Lieder in its highest state. In *An die untergehende Sonne*, which depicts the calm and beauty of a sunset, the peace of the scene is perfectly suggested by Janet's ethereal tone. In those two famous songs, *Gretchen am Spinnrad* and *Die junge Nonne*, one is perhaps accustomed to a lighter, less confident vocal characterisation but the searing power of the latter overcomes all reservations. Here we have the grand dramatic mezzo of Dido in *Les Troyens* in full flood; so too in the rarely encountered *Delphine*. This expansive piece—Richard Capell in his book on Schubert songs called it "an amorous woman's rhapsody"—now at last receives its due "with", as Desmond Shawe-Taylor commented, "a lightness and airiness in the piano part and a fervour in the singing that avoid all suggestion of clumsiness or excessive length". The more familiar *Das Mädchen*, with alternating minor-major modulations, ideally suggests the girl's doubts about her lover, and its muted sorrow is exactly reflected in this interpretation.

The lighter side of the singer's art comes to the fore in the satirical *Epistel an Herrn Josef Spaun* and *Die Männer sind Méchant*. Altogether these two discs are a treasure-house of mostly unfamiliar gems.

There is more undiscovered Schubert on Janet's two other Lieder recitals. On ASD2431, she retrieves *Am Grabe Anselmos*, a girl grieving over her dead lover, from oblivion as she has done at many 'live' recitals. In *Die Götter Griechenlands*, all the longing for a land of lost content is conjured up by her empty, sad tones. There is the requisite ecstasy at the end of *Auflösung*, mystery in the barcarolle, *Gondelfahrer*, where her *mezza voce* is delicate, and wistful, and naughty joyfulness in *Die Vögel*.

For the Wolf group on this disc, Janet switches, rightly, to a more straightforward less sophisticated style, and her chosen group from the Spanish Song Book are sensitively done, especially *Herr, was trägt der Boden hier*, where the two characters are imaginatively differentiated. Again there is some most beautiful *mezza voce* singing in Strauss's *Morgen* and *Die Nacht*, two of the composer's most memorable songs, and *Befreit* has noble intensity. *Heimliche Aufforderung* does not come off because it really calls for a man's voice; it is the only real failure on this enjoyable well-varied disc.

Janet's earliest Lieder disc, still available, can be said to have "made her name" as a recording artist. It was done for the small firm of Saga, which deserves credit for its foresight. Alec Robertson immediately recognised that a new Lieder singer of consequence had arrived on the musical scene. He wrote: "The last great British woman singer of Lieder was Muriel Foster, who died in 1937, having retired from the concert platform some years previously. Like Janet Baker, she was a mezzo-soprano, the voice which, because of its warmth and variety of colour, is perhaps the best vehicle for Schumann's song cycle; and it is Miss Foster's beauty of voice, musicianship, and powers of interpretation that Miss Baker seems to have inherited". He also said that her performance of Schumann's *Frauenliebe und Leben* was the finest performance (singer and pianist) the cycle had yet enjoyed. She suggests wonderfully the developing moods of the girl, from her adoring rapture, through the happiness of marriage and childbirth, to the desolation

Recording with Gerald Moore.
[EMI

With Sir Adrian Boult at a session for Brahms's 'Alto Rhapsody'. [EMI

of grievous loss, expressed marvellously—"Die Welt ist leer, ist leer" is unbearably moving—by the change of tone colour in the final songs. In the wrong hands, this cycle can become sentimental and mawkish; Janet avoids this entirely by her direct, unaffected approach, her perfect judgement of tempos, and her clean, easy tone. She is faithfully supported by Martin Isepp, who beautifully manages the modulation into the postlude and whose imagination always works together with the singer's.

Brahms and more unfamiliar Schubert (*Der Musensohn* excepted) fills the second side. Janet sings touchingly in *Die abgeblühte Linde*, freshly in *Heimliches Leben*, with panache in *Der Musensohn*. The undertow of melancholy in Brahms's *Die Mainacht* and *Die Nachtigall* is finely realised by both artists, but best of all here is *Von ewiger Liebe* in which as Alec Robertson put it "singer and pianist almost boil over" in their combined fervour.

Janet's only other Brahms to date is the *Alto Rhapsody*, recorded under Boult to go with his performance of the Second Symphony. The troubled mood of the opening sections is finely caught; the cup of bitterness seems full to overflowing, and this reflects Clara Schumann's remarks that "the piece seems to me neither more nor less than the expression of his own heart's anguish" on recognising his unhappy love for her daughter. The diction keenly seconds the voice at "Die Öde verschlingt ihn" and at "Menschenhass", with the consonants almost spat out. She even redeems the 'schmalzy' final section by her flowing, unforced, ethereal tone. She has also sung this work memorably at London concerts with Horenstein and Abbado.

In the programme with Abbado she also sang some of Mahler's Rückert settings, including *Um Mitternacht* (excluded at the concert). This has been coupled with Mahler's Fifth Symphony, more recently with *Sea Pictures* by Elgar. This, and her recordings of *Kindertotenlieder* and *Lieder eines fahrenden Gesellen*, were made with Barbirolli. Edward Greenfield wrote in *The Guardian* of the Rückert songs under Abbado: "Has anyone ever conveyed so subtly the unexpected marking 'Innig' on *Liebst du um Schönheit* and yet at the same time sung with a true glow of joy? When it came to the longest and profoundest of them *Ich bin der Welt abhanden gekommen*, here was an experience granted us only rarely in the concert hall, a whole audience spellbound by the merest thread of sound". The experience can be recalled to mind in the home on this lovely record. I used to treasure, still do, Kathleen Ferrier's *Ich atmet' einen Linden Duft* and *Ich bin der Welt* (so poignant in the context of the words and the singer's untimely death), but Janet Baker's more flexible voice and even subtler attention to the text gives her versions an added immediacy, an almost tactile feeling. Desmond Shawe-Taylor refers to her "sublime singing" on this disc.

The *Knaben Wunderhorn* songs, with Geraint Evans, was originally issued by Delysé in 1966; it was reissued by Decca in 1972. There is some rigidity in Wyn Morris's direction, and there are those who quarrel with the division of some of the songs between the two singers, a practice that is inclined to break the unity of the composition. These points hardly detract from the musicianship and keen-edged characterisation of Janet's contribution, which reaches its climax in "Wo die schönen Trompeten blasen", happily given to her alone although it is in the form of a dialogue. Here she moulds her line and varies her tone with the utmost sense of the spirit of this evocative song. Janet also contributed, charmingly, to the 1969 seventieth-birthday tribute to Gerald Moore with two Mahler songs from his earliest settings.

In the two cycles with Barbirolli, Janet is adept at reaching the true meaning of the texts, for instance when she darkens her tone as she leans into and gradually expands it on the word "Leide", precisely as Mahler indicated that he wanted this to be sung, at the end of the first song in the *Gesellen* group, and in the way she conveys the numbed sense of loss at the start of *Kindertotenlieder*. Then in the final moments of the *Gesellen* cycle, she differentiates even between *pp* and *ppp*. However, this all-embracing attention to detail is subordinate to the deeply felt projection of the text's and the music's inner thought expressed in the extraordinary understanding of words and phrasing. There must be reservations about Barbirolli's conducting. Admittedly he draws tender, beautifully moulded playing from the Hallé, but his self-evident love for the music led him into unnecessary *ritardandi* and pauses that themselves leave an unwanted sentimental impression.

Janet was to have recorded *Das Lied von der Erde* with George Szell, but he died before the project came to fruition. It is to be earnestly hoped that she will very soon add this to her recorded repertory.

Barbirolli's slow conducting also mars Janet's recordings of Berlioz's *Nuits d'été* and *Schéhérazade*. "Spectre de la Rose" in the Berlioz cycle is the worst sufferer. In any case no singer has ever quite managed to encompass every facet of the Berlioz cycle, where the composer called for different kinds of voices for each song. Janet transposes down *Villanelle* and loses something of the song's *leggero* quality, trying to compensate by a rather studied treatment of the text. In the other three songs, her usual intense involvement wins the day and only the occasional doubt about the pronunciation of the French 'e' and 'é' spoils her scrupulous treatment of the text. A mezzo may not be as ideal as a light soprano for the Ravel, especially for "Asie", but Janet Baker finds the right airy timbre for this cycle and one completely capitulates to the delicate sensuality of "L'Indifférent".

Some critics have also felt that a lighter voice is called for in many of the songs in Janet's French recital. Although it is true that we are perhaps more used to a brighter tone in *Chansons de Bilitis* and some of the Fauré items, I think an unprejudiced ear will find advantages in the warmer, more seductive tone Janet can bring into play. Here, I like particularly the stark despair of Fauré's *Prison*, the *joie de vivre* of his *Notre Amour* and the lovely line in *En Sourdine*. However, the *tour de force* on this disc is Duparc's *Phidylé*, where the repeats of "Repose, O Phidylé" are evocatively sung in a refined tone; its climax is truly tremendous. A man's song? Yes, but this interpretation overcomes that objection.

Earlier, Janet recorded a disc for Oiseau-Lyre of seldom-heard Ravel, Chausson and Delage. The whole recital is filled with sensual poetry, and Baker is unrestrained in the impassioned settings, helped by the excellent Melos Ensemble. The Mallarmé songs are sung with great beauty of tone, although the voice is too near the microphone. The *Chansons Madecasses*, superbly characterised, do call for a man's voice, especially the erotic "Nahandove". The overwhelming sadness of Chausson's *Chanson perpetuelle* is movingly conveyed; now Janet must give us his *Poème*, which she learnt only in 1972

Recording 'Nuits d'été' with Sir John Barbirolli. [EMI

for a concert with the Scottish National Orchestra, a very passionate, sorrowfully romantic interpretation that deserves a wider currency.

The two records of duets with Fischer-Dieskau, mementos of occasions at the Queen Elizabeth Hall and Festival Hall respectively, call for little special comment. Both singers respond sensitively to each other and to the needs of the text. My favourites are the Schumann group and the Brahms on the earlier record—Brahms's *Die Nonne und Der Ritter*, mysterious and dramatic, is superb—and the Lawes colloquies on the latter.

BRITISH ORATORIO AND SONG

Janet's outstanding performance in this field remains her Angel in *The Dream of Gerontius*. I think no other performance so clearly demonstrates the importance she attaches to her treatment of the words. This is not just a matter of clear diction—many singers can claim to have that—but of her deliberate yet never artificial emphasis on certain key ones, such as "hurrying" and "judge" which gives her reading of the familiar text an individuality and conviction above all others that I have ever heard. From her first hushed "Alleluias" through her meaningful description of St Francis's ordeal and the triumphant "Alleluia" with the high A easily taken to the rapt tenderness of the Angel's farewell, this is a great performance. Her contribution to Sir Adrian Boult's recording of Elgar's *The Music Makers* is sung with just as much attention to expression. She launches the Holst's *Choral Fantasia* with panache on the World Record Club disc of this strangely affecting work and is no less at home in Vaughan Williams's *Hodie*.

Duets with Fischer-Dieskau.
[*Reg Wilson*

At a playback of Elgar's 'Sea Pictures' with Barbirolli and producer Christopher Bishop.
[*EMI*

Of specifically solo works, I suppose *Sea Pictures* will remain a particular favourite; she redeems music that is not always first-rate by the composer's highest standards by her radiant singing. Her solo in Delius's *Songs of Sunset* is gloriously sung and much of the melancholy and languor of the music is conveyed as it is in the duet with John Shirley-Quirk, who also sings with noble commitment in *Cynara* on the same disc.

Of her two recitals, the later for HMV is much to be preferred, chiefly because of the more varied choice of music. However, the earlier one is not to be ignored, if only because it was the singer's first appearance on discs; the record was made in 1962, and the very first song, Vaughan Williams's *The Call* already has the Baker stamp on it—a freshly thought-out approach to text, a gleaming, vibrant tone, and faultless technique and musicianship. Indeed, it is the kind of recital that must have excited music clubs up and down the country in those early days. HQS1091 is an even more comprehensive compendium of Janet's art. In Campian's *Fain would I wed* the tone is all lightness, the words tripping off the tongue; in the same composer's *Oft have I sighed* it changes colour to suggest touching pathos. *Sleep, Adam, Sleep* by Purcell finds her in glowing voice and downright, evangelical form. In the same composer's *Lord, what is man?*, a favourite at Baker recitals, she is at once, passionate, dramatic and magnificently articulate. As on the Saga disc, she shows her affinity with modern (but not *too* modern) British composers. Stanford's original and evocative setting of Keats's ballad *La belle dame sans merci* and William Busch's *Rest* are well worth rescuing, but I wish Janet had chosen Delius's rather than Quilter's setting of Shelley's *Love's Philosophy*. Martin Isepp (on Saga) and Gerald Moore both provide their usual sympathetic support to the singer, seconding her with really pointed playing.

Finally, I should mention SEOM8, which provides a richly assorted sample of the many records already listed, not in every case my favourite choice but a splendid introduction, if needed, to this artist's work, showing as the note has it "a marvellous affinity with each and every composer she interprets".

As a postlude to this study of Janet's career and records, I should like to quote from the handsome booklet commemorating the presentation of the coveted Shakespeare Prize given by the FVS Foundation Hamburg to her in 1971. In the *Laudatio* on that occasion Professor Hajo Hinrichs said: "If I have to find a basic formula for Janet Baker's supremacy, as for instance Gerald Moore (in his book *Am I too Loud?*) found the word 'rhythm' to define Fischer-Dieskau, then I would choose here the word 'reality' with the additional meanings of 'recognise', 'comprehend', conceive', 'realise' . . . In Janet Baker's own words everything that she interprets 'must for that moment be reality'. That is to say, when she sings she has no intention of alluding to people, character, events from a safe distance. On the contrary, she does not stand remote from these things, but identifies herself with them. Nor is the text for her simply an object; she actually lives it just as she lives the characters that she interprets. Thereby we believe in her interpretation of them. If they are in love, so are we; if they are sad, so are we."

Receiving the Shakespeare Prize in Hamburg, 1971. [Foto Kramer

❧ Discography ❧

Compiled by Malcolm Walker

Record Categories

Index Letters	Numbers	Example	Type of Record
Roman Capitals	Roman	33CX1746	Mono LP
Bold Face Capitals	Bold	**SAX2393**	Stereo LP

Abbreviations

A.	Angel (USA)	Del.	Delysé (UK)	O-L.	Oiseau-Lyre (UK)
Ar.	Argo (UK)	E.	Everest (USA)	S.	Saga (UK)
C.	Columbia (UK)	H.	His Master's Voice (UK)	W.	World Record Club (UK)
D.	Decca (UK)	L.	London (USA)		

1961 January–February
A Midsummer Night's Dream (*Mendelssohn*)—incidental music
with Heather Harper, Chorus and Philharmonia Orchestra,
Otto Klemperer
   C.33CX1746/**SAX2393**; A.35881/**S35881**

1961 October
DIDO AND AENEAS (*Purcell*)—complete (title-role) with
Raimund Herincx, Patricia Clark, St Anthony Singers, English
Chamber Orchestra, Sir Anthony Lewis
   O-L.OL50216/**SOL60047**

1962
"AN ANTHOLOGY OF ENGLISH SONG"—The call;
Youth and Love (*Vaughan Williams*). A Thanksgiving; Her
Song (*Ireland*). A Piper (*Head*). This is a sacred city; Love is a
sickness (*Armstrong Gibbs*). The Cloths of Heaven; To the
Queen of my Heart (*Dunhill*). Balulalow; Youth (*Warlock*).
King David; Come sing and dance (*Howells*). Sleep. I will go
with my father a-ploughing (*Gurney*). Come, away, come
away, death; It was a lover and his lass (*Finzi*)—with Martin
Isepp (piano)
   S.XIP7013; S.XID5213/**STXID5213**

1963 February
Quattro Pezzi Sacri (*Verdi*) with Philharmonia Chorus and
Orchestra, Carlo Maria Giulini
   H.AN120/**SAN120**; A.36125/**S36125**

1963
Choral Fantasia, Op. 51 (*Holst*) with Ralph Downes (organ),
Purcell Singers, English Chamber Orchestra, Imogen Holst
   W.CM50/**SCM50**; E.SDBR3136; **HQS1260**

1964 December
DREAM OF GERONTIUS (*Elgar*)—complete with Richard
Lewis, Kim Borg, Ambrosian Singers, Sheffield Philharmonic
Chorus, Hallé Choir and Orchestra, Sir John Barbirolli
   H.ALP2101–2/**ASD648–9**; SLS770; A.3660/**S3660**

"GLORIOUS JOHN"—DREAM OF GERONTIUS (*Elgar*)
The Angel's Farewell with Ambrosian Singers, Sheffield
Philharmonic Choir, Hallé Choir and Orchestra, Sir John
Barbirolli
   H.**SLS796**

1965 January–February
Hodie (*Vaughan Williams*) with Richard Lewis, John Shirley-
Quirk, Bach Choir, Choristers of Westminster Abbey, London
Symphony Orchestra, David Willcocks
   C.33SX1782/**SCX3570**; A.36297/**S36297**

1965 July
HIPPOLYTE ET ARICIE (*Rameau*)—complete (Phaedra)
with John Shirley-Quirk, Robert Tear, Angela Hickey, Rae
Woodland, Edgar Fleet, Gerald English, Roger Stalman, Patricia
Blans, John Whitworth, Keith Erwen, John Noble, Jill Gomez,

Christopher Keyte, St Anthony Singers, English Chamber Orchestra, Sir Anthony Lewis

   O–L.OL286–8/**SOL286–8**

1965 August
Dixit Dominus (*Handel*)—with Teresa Zylis-Gara, Martin Lane, Robert Tear, John Shirley-Quirk, Choir of King's College, Cambridge, English Chamber Orchestra, David Willcocks

   H.ALP2262/**ASD2262**; A.36331/**S36331**

1965 August
Sea Pictures, Op. 37 (*Elgar*)—with London Symphony Orchestra, Sir John Barbirolli

   H.ALP2106/**ASD655**; A.**S36796**; H.**ASD2721**

1965 October
SAVITRI (*Holst*)—complete (title-role) with Robert Tear, Thomas Hemsley, Purcell Singers, English Chamber Orchestra, Imogen Holst

   Ar.NF6/**ZNF6**

1965
"LIEDER RECITAL"—Frauenliebe und Leben, Op. 42 (*Schumann*). Heimliches Lieben, D922; Minnelied, D429; Die Abgeblühte Linde, D514; Der Musensohn, D764 (*Schubert*). Die Mainacht, Op. 43 No. 2; Das Mädchen spricht, Op. 107 No. 3; Nachtigall, Op. 97 No. 1; Von ewiger Liebe, Op. 43 No. 1 (*Brahms*) with Martin Isepp (piano)

   S.XID5277/**STXID5277**

1966 February
Cantatas—No. 159: "Sehet, wir gehn hinauf gen Jerusalem"★; No. 170: "Vergnügte Ruh', beliebte Seelenlust" (*Bach*) — with Academy of St Martin-in-the-Fields, Neville Marriner. Item marked★ also with Robert Tear, John Shirley-Quirk, St Anthony Singers

   O–L.OL295/**SOL295**

1966 March
Des Knaben Wunderhorn (*Mahler*)—with Sir Geraint Evans, London Philharmonic Orchestra, Wyn Morris

   Del.ECB3177/**DS3177**; A.36380/**S36380**; D.**SDD–R326**

1966 June
"FRENCH SONGS" Trois Poèmes de Stephane Mallarmé*****; Chansons Madécasses (*Ravel*). Chanson Perpétuelle, Op. 37. (*Chausson*). Quatre Poèmes Hindous (*Delage*).—with Melos Ensemble. Item marked * conducted by Bernard Keeffe

   O–L.OL298/**SOL298**

1966 June, July and August
MESSIAH (*Handel*)—complete with Elizabeth Harwood, Robert Tear, Raimund Herincx, Ambrosian Singers, English Chamber Orchestra, Charles Mackerras

   H.HQM1052–4/**HQS1052–4**; SLS774; A.3705/**S3705**
   Excerpts from complete recording—H.**HQS1244**

1966 July
Cantatas—No. 82: "Ich habe genug"; No. 169: "Gott soll allein mein Herze haben"* (*Bach*)—with Bath Festival

Orchestra, Yehudi Menuhin. Item marked * also with Ambrosian Singers

   H.ALP2302/**ASD2302**; A.36419/**S36419**

1966 July
Gloria (*Vivaldi*); Magnificat† (*Pergolesi*)—with Elizabeth Vaughan, Choir of King's College, Cambridge, Academy of St Martin-in-the-Fields, David Willcocks. Item marked † also with Ian Partridge, Christopher Keyte

   Ar.RG505/**ZRG505**

1966 December
Music Makers, Op. 69 (*Elgar*)—with London Philharmonic Choir and Orchestra, Sir Adrian Boult

   H.ALP2311/**ASD2311**

1967 February
"A PAGEANT OF ENGLISH SONG: 1577–1961"
Come again (*Dowland*). Never love unless you can; Oft have I sighed; If thou longst so much to learn; Fain would I wed (*Campian*). Sleep, Adam, sleep, sleep; Lord, what is man? (*Purcell*). Tell me lovely shepherd (*Boyce arr. Poston*). My lovely Celia (*Monro*). Where the bee sucks (*Arne*)—with Martin Isepp (harpsichord), Robert Spencer (lute), Ambrose Gauntlett (viola da gamba) and Douglas Whittaker (flute). La Belle Dame sans Merci (*Stanford*). Proud Maisie; O Mistress Mine (*Parry*). Rest (*William Busch*). Pretty Ring Time (*Warlock*). Linden Lea (*Vaughan Williams*). The fields are full (*Gurney*). Corpus Christi Carol (*Britten*). Down by the Salley Gardens (*Ireland*). Love's Philosophy (*Quilter*)—with Gerald Moore (piano)

   H.**HQS1091**; A.**S36456**

1967 May and July
Lieder eines fahrenden Gesellen; Kindertotenlieder; Rückert Lieder—Ich bin der Welt abhanden gekommen (*Mahler*)—with Hallé Orchestra, Sir John Barbirolli

   H.**ASD2338**; A.**S36465**

1967 July
Cantata No. 80: "Ein' feste Burg ist unser Gott" (*Bach*)—with Elly Ameling, Theo Altmeyer, Hans Sotin, South German Madrigal Choir, Consortium Musicum, Wolfgang Gönnenwein

   H.**ASD2381**; A.**S36419**

1967 July
Cantatas—No. 79: "Gott, der Herr, ist Sonn' und Schild"; No. 148: "Bringet dem Herrn Ehre"; No. 149: "Man singet mit Freuden vom Sieg" (*Bach*)—with Elly Ameling, Theo Altmeyer, Hans Sotin, South German Madrigal Choir, Consortium Musicum, Wolfgang Gönnenwein

   H.**ASD2396**

1967 August and December
Les nuits d'été (*Berlioz*); Schéhérazade (*Ravel*)—with New Philharmonia Orchestra conducted by Sir John Barbirolli

   A.**S36505**; H.**ASD2444**

1967 October and November
MASS IN B MINOR, BWV244 (*Bach*)—with Agnes

Giebel, Nicolai Gedda, Hermann Prey, Franz Crass, BBC Chorus, New Philharmonia Orchestra, Otto Klemperer
  H.SAN195–7; A.S3730

1967 November
"LIEDER RECITAL"—Am Grabe Anselmos, D 504; Abendstern, D806; Die Vögel, D691; Strophe von Schiller, D677; Gondelfahrer, D808; Auflösung, D807 (*Schubert*).
Nun wandre Maria; Die ihr schwebet; Ach, des Knaben Augen; Herr, was trägt der Boden hier? (*Wolf*).
All mein Gedanken; Heimliche Aufforderung; Die Nacht; Morgen; Wiegenlied; Befreit; Allerseelen (*R. Strauss*)—with Gerald Moore (piano)
  H.ASD2431

1967 November and December
Ah! crudel nel pianto mio; Armida abbandonata (*Handel. ed. Leppard*)—with English Chamber Orchestra, Raymond Leppard
  H.ASD2468; A.S36569

1968 June
Songs of Sunset (*Delius*)—with John Shirley-Quirk, Liverpool Philharmonic Choir, Royal Liverpool Philharmonic Orchestra, Charles Groves
  H.ASD2437; A.S36603

1968 July
ELIJAH (*Mendelssohn*)—complete with Gwyneth Jones, Nicolia Gedda, Dietrich Fischer-Dieskau, Simon Woolf, Wandsworth School Boys' Choir, New Philharmonia Chorus and Orchestra, Rafael Frühbeck de Burgos
  H.SAN212–4; A.S3738; SLS935
  Excerpts from complete recording—H.ASD2609

1968 December
"A TRIBUTE TO GERALD MOORE" Frühlingsmorgen; Scheiden und Meiden (*Mahler*)—with Gerald Moore (piano)
  H.SAN255; A.S36640

1969 May
Magnificat in D major, BWV243 (*Bach*)—with Lucia Popp, Anne Pashley, Robert Tear, Thomas Hemsley, New Philharmonia Chorus and Orchestra, Daniel Barenboim
  H.ASD2533; A.S36615

1969 June and July
Salve Regina (*D. Scarlatti*).
L'INCORONAZIONE DI POPPEA: Disprezzata Regina; Addio Roma. Arianna's Lament (*Monteverdi*).
Cantata pastorale (*A. Scarlatti*)—with English Chamber Orchestra, Raymond Leppard
  H.ASD2615

1969 July
Rückert Lieder (*Mahler*)—with New Philharmonia Orchestra, Sir John Barbirolli
  H.ASD2519; SLS785; A.S3760; H.ASD2721; A.S36796

1969 July
"A FRENCH SONG RECITAL—Trois Chansons de Bilitis; Le Promenoir des Deux Amants (*Debussy*).

Au pays où se fait la Guerre; Phidylé (*Duparc*).
Automne; Prison; Soir; Fleur jetée; En Sourdine; Notre amour; Mai; Chanson de Pêcheur; Clair de lune (*Fauré*)——with Gerald Moore (piano)
  H.ASD2590

1969 September
LES TROYENS: Act 5 scenes 2 and 3†; La mort de Cléopatre (*Berlioz*)—with London Symphony Orchestra, Alexander Gibson. Item marked † with Bernadette Greevy, Keith Erwen, Gwynne Howell, Ambrosian Opera Chorus
  H.ASD2516; A.S36695

1969 September and October
LA DAMNATION DE FAUST (*Berlioz*)—complete (Marguerite) with Nicolai Gedda, Gabriel Bacquier, Pierre Thau, Paris Opera Chorus, Orchestre de Paris, Georges Prêtre
  H.SLS947; A.SCL3758

1969 August
(public performances at the Queen Elizabeth Hall, London)
"DUETS" Sound the trumpet; My dearest, my fairest; No, resistance is but vain; Shepherd, leave decoying (*Purcell*).
Er und Sie, Op. 78 No. 2; Wiegenlied, Op. 78 No. 4; Ich bin dein Baum, Op. 101 No. 3; Schön ist das Fest des Lenzes, Op. 37 No. 7; Herbstlied, Op. 43 No. 2; Tanzlied, Op. 78 No. 1 (*Schumann*).
Abschiedslied der Zugvögel, Op. 63 No. 2; Wie kann ich froh und lustig sein; Herbstlied, Op. 63 No. 4; Suleika und Hatem, Op. 8 No. 12 (*Mendelssohn*).
Heimatgedanken, Op. 16 No. 1; Verratene Liebe; Ich und du; Der beste Liebesbrief, Op. 16 No. 2 (*Cornelius*).
Die Nonne und der Ritter, Op. 28 No. 1; Vor der Tür, Op. 28 No. 2; Es rauschet das Wasser, Op. 28 No. 3; Der Jäger und sein Liebchen, Op. 28 No. 4 (*Brahms*)—with Dietrich Fischer-Dieskau (baritone), Daniel Barenboim (piano)
  H.ASD2553

1970 February
(public performance at the Royal Festival Hall, London)
"DUETS FROM THE ROYAL FESTIVAL HALL"
Tua Jesu dilecto (*Lilius*). Der Herr schauet vom Himmel; Verbum caro factum est, alleluia (*Schütz*). Christe, der Du bist Tag und Licht; Gott der Vater wohn uns bei (*Schein*). A Dialogue on a Kiss (*Henry Lawes*). A Dialogue between Charon and Philomel; A Dialogue between Daphne and Strephon (*William Lawes*). Giù nei Tartarei regni v'andrem madonna; Quando in calma ride il mare (*Handel*)—with Dietrich Fischer-Dieskau (baritone), Kenneth Heath (cello), George Malcolm (harpsichord)
  H.ASD2710; A.S36712

1970 July
Cantata No. 147; "Herz und Mund und Tat und Leben" (*Bach*)—with Elly Ameling, Ian Partridge, John Shirley-Quirk, Choir of King's College, Cambridge, Academy of St Martin-in-the-Fields, David Willcocks
  H.HQS1254

1970 July
THE RAPE OF LUCRETIA (*Britten*)—complete (title-role)
with Peter Pears, Heather Harper, John Shirley-Quirk, Bryan
Drake, Benjamin Luxon, Elizabeth Bainbridge, English
Chamber Orchestra, Benjamin Britten
    D.**SET**492–3; L.**OSA**1288
    Excerpts from complete recording—D.**SET**537

1970 August and December
"A SCHUBERT EVENING" Gretchen am Spinnrade,
D118; Suleika I (Was bedeutet die Bewegung?), D720;
Suleika II (Ach, um deine feuchten Schwingen), D717;
Schwestergruss, D762; Schlummerlied, D527; An die unter-
gehende Sonne, D457; Mignon I (Heiss mich nicht reden),
D877 No. 2; Mignon II (So lasst mich scheinen), D877 No. 3;
Mignon III (Nur wer die Sehnsucht), D877 No. 4; Mignon
Gesang (Kennst du das Land?), D321; Berthas Lied in der
Nacht, D653; Epistel an Herrn Josef von Spaun, D749; Ellen
I (Raste, Krieger!), D837; Ellen II (Jäger, ruhe von der Jagd),
D838; Ellen III (Ave Maria), D839; Claudine von Villa Bella,
D239—No. 3: Hin und wieder; No. 6: Liebe schwärmt; An
die Nachtigall, D497; Des Mädchens Klage, D6; Delphine,
D857; Wiegenlied, D867; Die Männer sind mechant, D866
No. 3; Wiegenlied (Schlafe, schlafe!), D498; Iphigenia, D573;
Das Mädchen, D652; Die junge Nonne, D828—with Gerald
Moore (piano)
    H.**SLS**812

1970 September
Mass in C major, Op. 86 (*Beethoven*)—with Elly Ameling,
Theo Altmeyer, Marius Rintzler, New Philharmonia Chorus
and Orchestra, Carlo Maria Giulini
    H.**ASD**2661; A.**S**36775

1970 December
OWEN WINGRAVE (*Britten*)—complete (Kate Julian) with
Benjamin Luxon, John Shirley-Quirk, Heather Harper,
Peter Pears, Sylvia Fisher, Jennifer Vyvyan, Nigel Douglas,
Wandsworth School Boys' Choir, English Chamber Orchestra,
Benjamin Britten
    D.**SET**501–2; L.**OSA**1291

1970 December
Alto Rhapsody, Op. 53 (*Brahms*)—with John Alldis Choir,
London Philharmonic Orchestra, Sir Adrian Boult
    H.**ASD**2746

1971 July
Requiem Mass No. 19 in D minor, K626 (*Mozart*)—with
Sheila Armstrong, Nicolai Gedda, Dietrich Fischer-Dieskau,
John Alldis Choir, English Chamber Orchestra, Daniel
Barenboim
    H.**ASD**2788

1971 August
LA CALISTO (*Cavalli ed. Leppard*)—complete performing
edition with Marjorie Biggar, Enid Hartle, Teresa Cahill,
Ugo Trama, Peter Gottlieb, Ileana Cotrubas, James Bowman,
Hugues Cuénod, Janet Hughes, Federico Davia, Owen
Brannigan, Teresa Kubiak, Ilsa Brodie, Glyndebourne Festival
Opera Chorus, London Philharmonic Orchestra, Raymond
Leppard
    Ar.**ZNF**11–12

JANET BAKER—Sampler record
Fain would I wed (*Campian*) **February 1967.**
Lord, what is man? (*Purcell*) **February 1967.**
Cantata No. 82—Ich habe genug (*Bach*) **July 1966.**
Italian Cantata No. 1—"Ah crudel, nel pianto mio"—Non
sdegnerai d'amar . . . Di quel bel (*Handel ed. Leppard*) **November–
December 1967**
ELIJAH—O rest in the Lord (*Mendelssohn*) **July 1968.**
Morgen (*Richard Stauss*) **November 1967.**
Clair de lune (*Fauré*) **July 1969.**
Les nuits d'été—Villanelle **August 1967**; LES TROYENS:
Pluton . . . semble . . . m'etre propice (*Berlioz*). **September 1969**
Rückert Lieder—No. 4: Ich bin der Welt abhanden gekom-
men (*Mahler*) **May 1967**—with various accompaniments
    H.**SEOM**8

October 1972